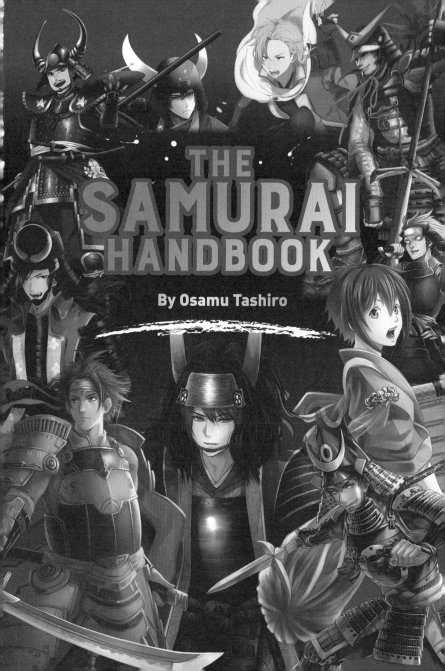

THE SAMURAI HANDBOOK

By Osamu Tashiro

By Osamu Tashiro
Written by Noriyuki Irisawa
Translated by Peter Porcino
Edited by Nancy Ellwood and Sarah Parvis
First U.S. edition design by Georgia Rucker

Cover Illustration by Aohito
Interior Illustrations by Akami (pages 21, 55), Akitsuka Yurai (pages 35, 115),
Amagasa (page 94), Aohito (pages 12, 32, 42, 50, 102), Babovich (page 26),
Fukayama Hitaki (page 128), Hachi (pages 45, 81, 123, 140), Hinoto (page 75),
Ishii Risa (page 44), Kakumayu (page 23), Kikuya Kei (pages 40, 126), Kikuya Shiro
(pages 46, 78, 90), Kiriko (page 98), KNDY (page 18), Kosuke (page 34), Matsuri
(page 138), miska (pages 82, 106), Miyamoto Satoru (pages 24, 66, 76, 110, 130),
Miyoshi Norikatsu (page 68), Mizoremeshi (page 88), Motsuru (page 129), Nachiko
(pages 64, 92, 96, 120, 132), Nakayasu Tsubasa (page 36), Nikaido Aya (page 95),
Nkyoku (page 114), Nozomi (pages 15, 89), Sato Aoi (page 37), siki (page 112), Sue
Kouhei (page 70), Suizu Keiri (pages 122, 134), Suzumoto (pages 27, 107), Tomida
Tomomi (page 104), Totomaru (pages 54, 117), Tsuboi Ryohei (pages 16, 52, 62,
86), Tsuchinoko (page 19), Uzuki Yohane (pages 20, 71, 135), Watari (pages 30, 80),
Yamada Shibu (pages 116, 139, 143), Yamanaka Kanako (pages 48, 113), Yonekawa
Sho (page 142), Yukihama (pages 74, 141), Yuu (page 22).

Gakken Plus Co., Ltd., Japan
The Samurai Handbook by Osamu Tashiro
ISBN 978-4-05-621063-7
Originally published by Gakken in Japan as
Sengoku Busho Visual Daihyakka © 2017
Copyright © Gakken Plus 2018

gakkenplusna.com
10 9 8 7 6 5 4 3 2 1
PRINTED IN CHINA, AUGUST 2018

CONTENTS

HOW TO USE THIS BOOK

Clan or Army Affiliation

The book highlights 11 clans: their leaders, trusted advisers, retainers (the fighters pledged to them), and the warriors they clashed with. Each clan is assigned a color, so you know at a glance which group each samurai belongs to.

Name

The samurai's name in English and Japanese

Family Crest

The design seen on the samurai's armor and battle flags

Chief of the Heavenly Kings,
His War Cry Rang Out Over Battles

SHIBATA KATSUIE

Born: 1522 (?)
Died: 1583
Died at age 62 (?) by his own hand
Birthplace: Owari Province (present-day Aichi Prefecture)
Father: Shibata Katsuyoshi (?)
Wife: Oichi
Son: Shibata Katsutoshi

Main Base
Kitanosho Castle (Fukui)

Shibata Katsuie earned the nickname "Charging Shibata" by always yelling "Charge!" from the front lines as he leapt into battle. He was a loyal and brave servant of Oda Nobunaga. His willingness to hurl himself headlong into battle earned him great respect, and he became the leader of Nobunaga's four highest retainers: the "Four Heavenly Kings."

However, among these heavenly kings was Akechi Mitsuhide, the man who betrayed Nobunaga at Honnoji Temple. Nobunaga's death left a power vacuum in the Oda clan. Toyotomi Hideyoshi avenged his master's death by killing Mitsuhide and assuming leadership of the clan. Katsuie challenged Hideyoshi for leadership in two battles, but he was defeated at Kitanosho Castle. There, he and his wife, Oichi (Nobunaga's younger sister), took their own lives.

The Pot Chopper

There is a famous story from when the Rokkaku clan laid siege to a castle that Katsuie held. The Rokkaku cut off water to the castle and sent messengers urging Katsuie to surrender. After calmly sending the messengers away, he gave the remaining water to his soldiers and broke all the clay water pots with his bare hands. Their only chance for survival was to break the siege, so the soldiers rode out and won the battle. Nobunaga gave Katsuie the name "Shibata Pot Chopper."

Fighting Strength
Luck — Leadership
Humanity — Willpower
Intelligence

Known as "The Demon Shibata" for his otherworldly strength, Katsuie was a loyal servant of the Oda clan.

16 / 17

Biographical Box

Look here to find the soldier's year of birth and death, and the cause of death. You will also discover where he was born, the names of notable family members, and the geographical area where he was based.

Battle Flag

A picture of the flag the samurai wore on his back when he charged into battle

Fun Facts!

Fun facts and anecdotes about the lives of colorful samurai

What a Mouthful! A Note on Pronunciations

Japanese names might look long and weird—or short and weird—to you. But they're actually really easy to pronounce. Unlike in English, in Japanese the vowels A, E, I, O, U are always pronounced the same, no matter what letters come before or after them.

A is always "ah" like in *pasta*.

E is "eh" like in *pet*.

I is "ee" like in *see*.

O is just like you'd think: *oh*.

U is "oo" like in *moon*.

Remember that when you see a name like Sue or Date, you're not suing anyone or asking someone to go to the movies. Both names are two syllables: *su-eh* and *dah-teh*.

Samurai Portrait

A drawing of what each samurai or general might have looked like setting off for battle

Regions of Japan

Here are the major geographical areas of Japan.

Tohoku Region

Chubu Region

Kanto Region

Chugoku Region

Kinki Region

Kyushu Region

Shikoku Region

He's How Old?! A Note on Ages

The samurai's age at death is displayed using the ancient Japanese system of counting. In this system, a child is considered one year old when he or she is born. (The baby is "in its first year.") Every time January 1 comes around, another year is added to a person's age. (He is in his second year, third year, etc.) This is why the ages in this book appear to be one higher than they would be in our modern counting system.

Samurai Stats

Six traits that no samurai can live without. Some make you a fearsome warrior. Some make you a noble leader. Some make you a compassionate victor. Not everyone has them in equal measure, just like not everyone does equally well on the battlefield or at the negotiating table.

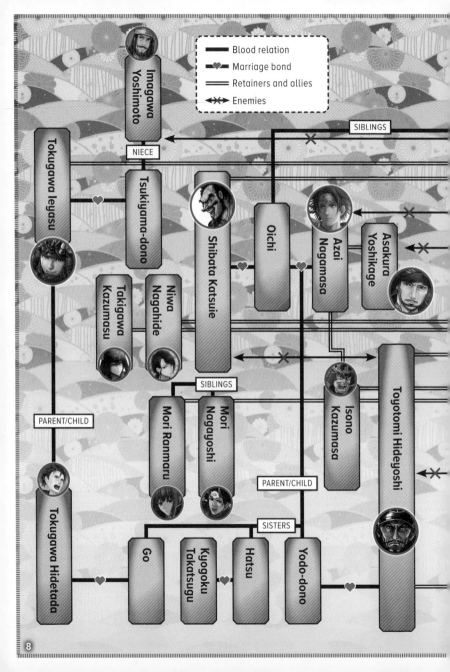

Legend
- ▬▬ Blood relation
- ♥▬ Marriage bond
- ══ Retainers and allies
- ◄►◄► Enemies

Imagawa Yoshimoto

SIBLINGS

NIECE

Tokugawa Ieyasu

Tsukiyama-dono

Shibata Katsuie

Oichi

Azai Nagamasa

Asakura Yoshikage

Takigawa Kazumasu

Niwa Nagahide

Mori Ranmaru

Mori Nagayoshi

SIBLINGS

Isono Kazumasa

Toyotomi Hideyoshi

PARENT/CHILD

Tokugawa Hidetada

PARENT/CHILD

Go

Kyogoku Takatsugu

Hatsu

Yodo-dono

SISTERS

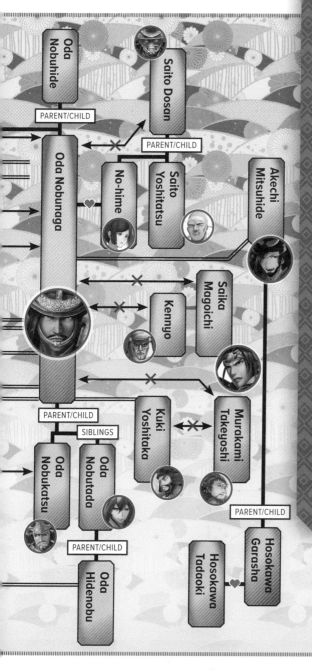

CHAPTER 1

THE ODA CLAN

AND THEIR RELATIONS

Meet those who helped Oda Nobunaga in his bid for the throne— and those who opposed him with all their might.

Oda Nobuhide

Saito Dosan

PARENT/CHILD

Oda Nobunaga

PARENT/CHILD

No-hime

Saito Yoshitatsu

Akechi Mitsuhide

Saika Magoichi

Kennyo

Murakami Takeyoshi

Kuki Yoshitaka

PARENT/CHILD

SIBLINGS

Oda Nobukatsu

Oda Nobutada

PARENT/CHILD

Hosokawa Garasha

Hosokawa Tadaoki

PARENT/CHILD

Oda Hidenobu

Map of Feudal Japan
1570–1573
Introducing...
NOBUNAGA!

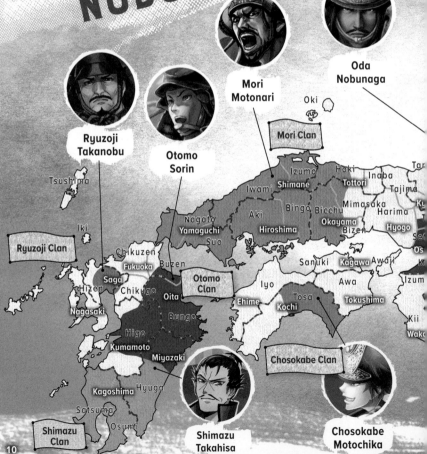

Ryuzoji
Takanobu

Otomo
Sorin

Mori
Motonari

Oda
Nobunaga

Oki

Mori Clan

Tsushima

Izumo
Hoki
Inaba
Tar
Tottori
Tajima
Iwami
Shimane
Mimasaka
Ku
Bingo
Bicchu
Harima
T
Nagato
Aki
Okayama
Yamaguchi
Hiroshima
Bizen
Hyogo
Suo
Iki
Se
Os
Chikuzen
Sanuki
Kagawa
Awaji
K
Ryuzoji Clan
Fukuoka
Buzen
Izum
Saga
Iyo
Awa
Hizen
Chikugo
Otomo
Ehime
Tosa
Tokushima
Nagasaki
Clan
Kochi
Oita
Kii
Bungo
Higo
Wako
Kumamoto
Chosokabe Clan
Miyazaki
Kagoshima
Hyuga
Satsuma
Osumi
Shimazu
Clan
Shimazu
Takahisa
Chosokabe
Motochika

10

The lords of every domain have their eyes set on the throne in Kyoto. The favorite contender is Imagawa Yoshimoto—that is, until he is defeated by the upstart Oda Nobunaga. Think fast, because the map of feudal Japan will be redrawn with every new battle.

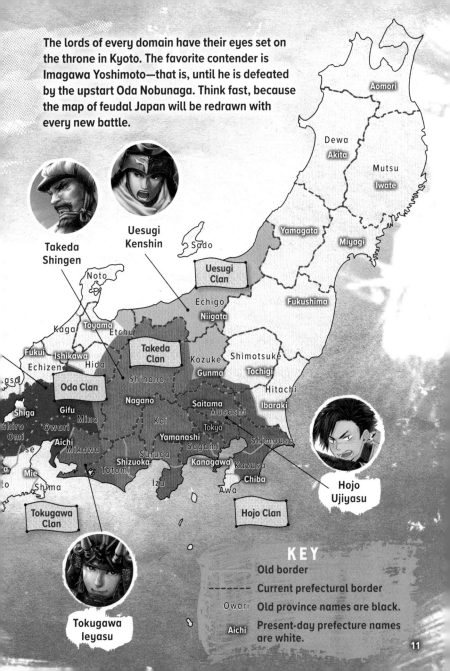

Takeda Shingen

Uesugi Kenshin

Aomori

Dewa
Akita

Mutsu
Iwate

Yamagata

Miyagi

Sado

Uesugi Clan

Echigo
Niigata

Fukushima

Noto

Kaga
Toyama
Etchu

Ishikawa
Fukui
Echizen
Hida

Takeda Clan

Kozuke
Shimotsuke

Gunma
Tochigi

Oda Clan

Shinano

Hitachi

Shiga
Gifu
Mino

Nagano

Saitama
Musashi

Ibaraki

Owari
Omi
shiro

Aichi
Mikawa

Kai

Tokyo

Ise
Mie

Shizuoka
Totomi

Yamanashi
Suruga

Sagami
Kanagawa

Shimousa
Shimousa

asa

Kazusa

Shima

Izu

Chiba

Awa

Hojo Ujiyasu

Tokugawa Clan

Hojo Clan

Tokugawa Ieyasu

KEY

—— Old border

------- Current prefectural border

Owari Old province names are black.

Aichi Present-day prefecture names are white.

11

Poised to unify the nation, he had the ambition to rule!

ODA NOBUNAGA

As a child, Oda Nobunaga spent much of his time half naked, wearing a hakama robe made of tiger skin, with a gourd hanging from his waist. This strange outfit earned him some cruel nicknames, like "the great fool of Owari." But when Nobunaga was just 18 years old, his father died. Nobunaga assumed the mantle of leader of the Oda clan and was reborn as a great warrior.

After defeating Imagawa Yoshimoto at the Battle of Okehazama, Nobunaga became famous overnight. He entered into an alliance with Tokugawa Ieyasu. From there he defeated the Saito clan and took control of Mino Province. The road to Kyoto—and the seat of power to control the nation— was Nobunaga's for the taking.

Nobunaga took Kyoto, but he was soon surrounded by his enemies: Asakura Yoshikage, Azai Nagamasa, and Takeda Shingen. He also had angry warrior monks to contend with: the monks of Enryakuji Temple on Mt. Hieizan in Kyoto and the monks of Ishiyama Honganji Temple. Undaunted, Nobunaga smashed through the encircling armies, defeating Nagamasa at the Battle of Anegawa River, and razed the Hieizan Temple complex. He overthrew the Muromachi shoguns in Kyoto and, at Ichijodani Castle, slew his rival Yoshikage.

Born: 1534
Died: 1582
Died at age 49 by his own hand
Birthplace: Owari Province (present-day Aichi Prefecture)
Father: Oda Nobuhide
Children: Oda Nobutada, Oda Nobukatsu

Main Base

Azuchi Castle (Shiga)

continued on page 14

織田信長

Fighting Strength

Luck

Leadership

Humanity

Willpower

Intelligence

Known for his decisiveness and his foresight, Nobunaga could also be ruthless. His rallying cry was, "Take the world by force!"

1	2	3	4	5	6	7	8
Oda Clan	Takeda, Uesugi, and Hojo Clans	Toyotomi Clan	Mori Clan	Date Clan	Shimazu, Otomo, and Chosokabe Clans	Tokugawa Clan	Other Samurai

ODA NOBUNAGA continued

Nobunaga went head-to-head with the Takeda clan at the Battle of Nagashino. He led his corps of musketeers against Takeda Katsuyori's cavalry.

All that remained were the warrior monks besieged at the Ishiyama Honganji Temple. When the Mori clan's navy tried to resupply the monks with food, Nobunaga destroyed the flotilla with Kuki Yoshitaka's ironclad warship. Nobunaga now controlled the Osaka Bay, and Ishiyama Honganji Temple soon fell.

Nobunaga's dream of uniting the nation under one ruler had come one step closer to reality. His next strategy was to send Toyotomi Hideyoshi to the heartlands to the east to subdue the Mori clan.

In 1582, Nobunaga decided to reinforce his troops. In June, he camped at Kyoto's Honnoji Temple with a small group of soldiers. They came under attack. The attackers were led by Akechi Mitsuhide, one of Nobunaga's own retainers. Nobunaga fought to the bitter end, but when he saw that all was lost, he took his own life.

Betrayal

Nobody knows for sure why Nobunaga was betrayed by Mitsuhide, one of his most adept retainers. When he learned that Mitsuhide was leading the attack, Nobunaga is reported to have said, "He's come at last." Had Nobunaga sensed the danger all along?

An Incredible Marksman
TAKIGAWA KAZUMASU

滝川一益

Born: 1525
Died: 1586
Died at age 62 from illness

One of the four retainers who were known as Nobunaga's "Four Heavenly Kings," Takigawa Kazumasu earned his reputation at the Battle of Nagashino when he gunned down the powerful Takeda Katsuyori, among others. After Nobunaga's death, Kazumasu surrendered to Toyotomi Hideyoshi, who had just slain Shibata Katsuie at the Battle of Shizugatake. Kazumasu retired and became a Buddhist monk.

Fighting Strength

Luck

Leadership

Humanity

Willpower

Intelligence

Kazumasu was an expert strategist, known for his intelligence, willpower, and marksmanship.

| 1 Oda Clan | 2 Takeda, Uesugi, and Hojo Clans | 3 Toyotomi Clan | 4 Mori Clan | 5 Date Clan | 6 Shimazu, Otomo, and Chosokabe Clans | 7 Tokugawa Clan | 8 Other Samurai |

Chief of the Heavenly Kings, His War Cry Rang Out Over Battles

SHIBATA KATSUIE

Born: 1522 (?)
Died: 1583
Died at age 62 (?)
by his own hand
Birthplace:
Owari Province
(present-day Aichi
Prefecture)
Father: Shibata
Katsuyoshi (?)
Wife: Oichi
Son: Shibata
Katsutoshi

Main Base

Kitanosho Castle
(Fukui)

Shibata Katsuie earned the nickname "Charging Shibata" by always yelling "Charge!" from the front lines as he leapt into battle. He was a loyal and brave servant of Oda Nobunaga. His willingness to hurl himself headlong into battle earned him great respect, and he became the leader of Nobunaga's four highest retainers: the "Four Heavenly Kings."

However, among these heavenly kings was Akechi Mitsuhide, the man who betrayed Nobunaga at Honnoji Temple. Nobunaga's death left a power vacuum in the Oda clan. Toyotomi Hideyoshi avenged his master's death by killing Mitsuhide and assuming leadership of the clan. Katsuie challenged Hideyoshi for leadership in two battles, but he was defeated at Kitanosho Castle. There, he and his wife, Oichi (Nobunaga's younger sister), took their own lives.

The Pot Chopper

There is a famous story from when the Rokkaku clan laid siege to a castle that Katsuie held. The Rokkaku cut off water to the castle and sent messengers urging Katsuie to surrender. After calmly sending the messengers away, he gave the remaining water to his soldiers and broke all the clay water pots with his bare hands. Their only chance for survival was to break the siege, so the soldiers rode out and won the battle. Nobunaga gave Katsuie the name "Shibata Pot Chopper."

柴田勝家

Fighting Strength

Luck

Leadership

Humanity

Willpower

Intelligence

Known as "the Demon Shibata" for his otherworldly strength, Katsuie was a loyal servant of the Oda clan.

17

Anything for Nobunaga
MORI NAGAYOSHI

森長可

**Born: 1558
Died: 1584
Died at age 27 in battle**

Fighting Strength

Luck

Leadership

Humanity

Willpower

Intelligence

Feared as a "Demon Warrior," Nagayoshi fought bravely in the face of certain death at the Battle of Komaki and Nagakute.

Mori Nagayoshi became head of the Mori clan at age 13 and served as one of Oda Nobunaga's retainers. He showed his valor in hard-fought battles against the Takeda and Uesugi clans.

After Nobunaga's death, Nagayoshi served under Toyotomi Hideyoshi, clashing with the allied forces of Oda Nobukatsu (Nobunaga's son) and Tokugawa Ieyasu. During the Battle of Komaki and Nagakute, Nagayoshi was slain.

MORI RANMARU

森蘭丸

**Born: 1565
Died: 1582
Died at age 18 in battle**

Fighting Strength

Luck

Leadership

Humanity

Willpower

Intelligence

A lover of learning, Ranmaru studied martial arts to protect his lord.

The younger brother of Mori Nagayoshi, Mori Ranmaru was Oda Nobunaga's personal attendant. Known for his youthful good looks, he died fighting beside his lord at Honnoji Temple.

An Untimely Death at the Hands of the Betrayer

ODA NOBUTADA

Born: 1557
Died: 1582
Died at age 26 by his own hand

織田信忠

Oda Nobutada followed his father Oda Nobunaga on campaigns. After defeating the Takeda clan, he was expected to be successor to the lordship of the Oda clan. But after his father's death, Nobutada made his last stand at Kyoto's Nijo Castle. When it was clear that victory would belong to Akechi Mitsuhide, the young Nobutada took his own life.

Fighting Strength

Luck

Leadership

Humanity

Willpower

Intelligence

With the military skill to overthrow the Takeda clan, Nobutada had a bright future. He died too soon.

"The next leader of the Oda clan is me!"
ODA NOBUKATSU

織田信雄

Born: 1558
Died: 1630
Died at age 73 from illness

Oda Nobukatsu was Oda Nobunaga's second son. After the betrayal at Honnoji Temple, Toyotomi Hideyoshi backed Oda Nobutada's son as the next leader of the Oda clan instead of Nobukatsu. To combat Hideyoshi, Nobukatsu made an alliance with Tokugawa Ieyasu. Together they fought against Hideyoshi. Nobukatsu eventually made peace with Hideyoshi and agreed to serve the new leader of the clan.

Fighting Strength

Luck

Leadership

Humanity

Willpower

Intelligence

Nobukatsu had the ambition to seek power, but not the strength to seize it.

A Cool and Collected Demon Warrior

NIWA NAGAHIDE

Ⓧ

丹羽長秀

**Born: 1535
Died: 1585
Died at age 51 from illness**

Niwa Nagahide was a rare combination: a fearsome warrior and a calm, capable politician. He made himself so important to the daily operation of the clan that Oda Nobunaga named him "Lieutenant Rice," meaning that he was as essential to their way of life as a bowl of rice.

After the betrayal at Honnoji Temple, Nagahide joined Toyotomi Hideyoshi's campaign to unite the nation.

Fighting Strength

Luck

Leadership

Humanity

Willpower

Intelligence

One of Oda's "Four Heavenly Kings," Nagahide was a jack of all trades— and master of every one.

Best Bowman in Tokai
IMAGAWA YOSHIMOTO

今川義元

Born: 1519
Died: 1560
Died at age 42 in battle

Fighting Strength

Luck

Leadership

Humanity

Willpower

Intelligence

Strong and clever, Yoshimoto aspired to unite the nation under his own banner.

Known as the best bowman in the Tokai region (present-day Aichi, Gifu, Mie, and Shizuoka prefectures), Imagawa Yoshimoto was a favorite to unite the nation under his own rule. To this end, he joined forces with the Takeda and Hojo clans and marched on Kyoto at the head of a great army. But before he could get there, his forces were surprised by Oda Nobunaga while they rested. Yoshimoto was killed in the battle.

"I will not forgive Nobunaga's betrayal!"

AZAI NAGAMASA

Born: 1545
Died: 1573
Died at age 29
by his own hand
Birthplace:
Omi Province
(present-day Shiga
Prefecture)
Wife: Oichi
Daughters:
Chacha (Yodo-dono),
Hatsu, Go

Main Base

Odani Castle
(Shiga)

The Azai clan had been close with the Asakura clan for a long time.

Azai Nagamasa's wife was Oda Nobunaga's younger sister, and the two men had formed an alliance that extended to the Asakura clan. Despite this, Nobunaga attacked Asakura Yoshikage. This move enraged Nagamasa, who felt he was honor bound to come to his friend's aid. He attacked Nobunaga's forces from the rear, but Nobunaga managed to escape.

The Azai and Asakura armies met Nobunaga's troops at the Battle of Anegawa River, but they suffered a devastating defeat. Nagamasa retreated with his remaining troops to his home base at Odani Castle. Besieged by Nobunaga, he fought to the bitter end, and there he took his own life.

Nagamasa's Wife and Daughters

Nagamasa's wife, Oichi, was known as the most beautiful woman of the age. The couple had three daughters. The oldest, Chacha, later became Toyotomi Hideyoshi's concubine. She gave birth to a son, Hideyori, who became Hideyoshi's heir.

24

浅井長政

Fighting
Strength

Luck

Leadership

Humanity

Willpower

Intelligence

Both wise and brave, Nagamasa died young,
defending the honor of his friend.

"I won't bow down to Nobunaga!"
ASAKURA YOSHIKAGE

Born: 1533
Died: 1573
Died at age 41 by his own hand

Asakura Yoshikage was the 11th lord of the Asakura clan. When Oda Nobunaga conquered Kyoto and demanded that the Asakuras submit to his rule, Yoshikage ignored him. So Nobunaga sent his forces to attack the clan. With the help of Azai Nagamasa, the Asakuras defended their lands for a time. But, at the Battle of Anegawa River, they were defeated. To add insult to injury, Yoshikage was betrayed by his own retainer. He took his own life.

Fighting Strength

Luck

Leadership

Humanity

Willpower

Intelligence

Yoshikage fortified his home base at Ichijodani Castle, but had little will to wage war.

26

✸ Death Means Nothing to the Sanada Clan

Just like the Ancient Greeks believed you had to cross the River Styx to get to the land of the dead, the feudal Japanese believed you had to cross the Sanzu River. And what's more, you had to pay the boatman six coins to take you there. To show that they were not afraid of dying in battle, the soldiers of the Sanada put those six coins on the clan's crest, which they carried on flags into battle.

✸ Nobunaga's Famous Fingernails

Mori Ranmaru was one of Oda Nobunaga's personal attendants, and he was famous for his close attention to detail. To test this, Nobunaga cut the nails on nine of his fingers. He put the clippings on a folding fan and told Ranmaru to throw them outside. Ranmaru left the room, then returned a minute later and began looking on the ground to see if he had dropped the 10th fingernail clipping somewhere!

✸ Too Heavy for a Quick Getaway?

Ryuzoji Takanobu was too big to ride a horse, so he had his men carry him into battle on a platform. At the Battle of Okitanawate, the enemy quickly discovered the position of this platform. The platform was so heavy Takanobu's soldiers couldn't move very quickly, and as a result Takanobu was shot while trying to flee.

The Most Intimidating Helmets Ever to See Battle

Samurai helmets are not just for keeping your noggin from getting smashed. Samurai generals flaunted their strength with their helmets as much as with their swords.

Private collection

Honda Tadakatsu

What do you get when you combine a stag's antlers with the head of a lion? One fearsome work of art.

Kuroda Nagamasa

Bring on the buffalo! You better make room when Nagamasa charges.

Collection of the Fukuoka City Museum/Image: Fukuoka City Museum, DNPartcom/Photo by Fujimoto Kempachi

Todo Takatora

Wide load. Not all helmets are created equal!

Collection of the Iga City Board of Education

Based on ancient Chinese helmet designs, the wide wings are unmistakable on the battlefield.

Collection of the Sendai City Museum

Collection of the Tachibana Museum

Rooster's tail feathers

Uesugi Kenshin

This helmet is believed to have been Uesugi Kenshin's. It showed a god's face in three directions!

Tachibana Muneshige

You can't cut him if your sword just slides off the circle on his helmet, right?

Satake Yoshishige

A caterpillar with . . . feathers? It's not so funny when Yoshishige attacks.

Collection of the Akita City Satake Historical Center

29

Bows and Arrows

Ever since samurai first appeared in Japan more than 1,000 years ago, the bow and arrow has been the most common weapon found on the battlefield.

Arrowhead

There are holes in the turnip-shaped arrowhead that make these arrows whistle.

Turnip Arrowhead

Forked Arrowhead

Needle Arrowhead

"Turnip-head" arrows were used primarily for ceremonial archery or to mark the start of a battle. They made a low whistling sound when released.

Shaft

Fletching

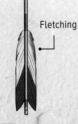

Motojiro

Kirifu

Nakaguro

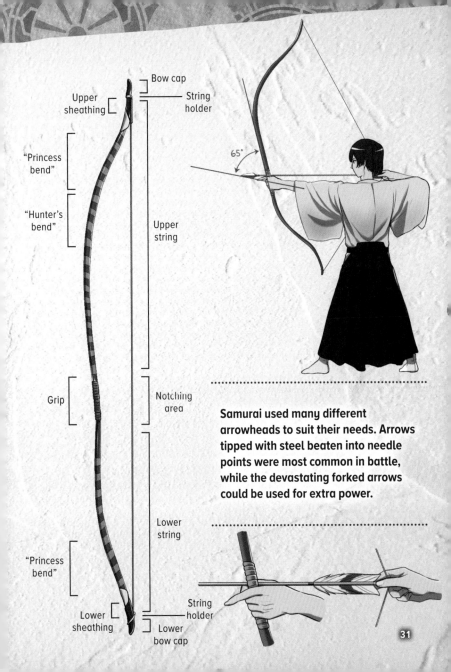

Bow cap

String holder

Upper sheathing

"Princess bend"

"Hunter's bend"

Upper string

65°

Grip

Notching area

Samurai used many different arrowheads to suit their needs. Arrows tipped with steel beaten into needle points were most common in battle, while the devastating forked arrows could be used for extra power.

Lower string

"Princess bend"

String holder

Lower sheathing

Lower bow cap

1	2	3	4	5	6	7	8
Oda Clan	Takeda, Uesugi, and Hojo Clans	Toyotomi Clan	Mori Clan	Date Clan	Shimazu, Otomo, and Chosokabe Clans	Tokugawa Clan	Other Samurai

Captain of the Saika Mercenaries
SAIKA MAGOICHI

Born: 1534 (?)
Died: 1589 (?)
Died at age 56 (?) from illness (?)
Birthplace: Kii Province (present-day Wakayama Prefecture)
Family: Unknown

Main Base

Saika Castle (Wakayama)

Saika Magoichi was the leader of the Saika mercenary clan. Mercenaries do not follow a single lord but instead are paid to go to battle where they are needed. The Saika clan were so renowned for their battle skills that other armies had a saying about them: "As allies, you're sure to win. As enemies, you're sure to die."

Because so many of the Saika clan were devout Buddhists, they joined forces with the monks at Ishiyama Honganji Temple in Osaka and fought against Oda Nobunaga for 10 years. This conflict became known as the Battle of Ishiyama Honganji.

No matter how large an army Nobunaga fielded against the Saika, the mercenaries' muskets always thwarted his troops. Finally Nobunaga decided he would take the fight to their home base in Kii Province. Both sides struggled to maintain territory. Meanwhile, the exhausted monks back in Osaka finally surrendered to Nobunaga. Since the monks were their allies, this meant that the Saika's fight was over too.

After Nobunaga's death, Magoichi fought on the side of Toyotomi Hideyoshi.

雑賀孫一
（さい）（か）（まご）（いち）

Fighting Strength

Luck

Leadership

Humanity

Willpower

Intelligence

Magoichi was the leader of a corps of marksmen who fought Nobunaga's army for 10 years.

The Pirate Captain Who Controlled the Inland Sea
MURAKAMI TAKEYOSHI

Born: 1533
Died: 1604
Died at age 72 from illness

村上武吉

Murakami Takeyoshi was one of the top captains of the dreaded Murakami pirates who ruled the Seto Inland Sea. At the Battle of Itsukushima, he allied with Mori Motonari and Kobayakawa Takakage to smash the host assembled there by Sue Harukata. Takeyoshi's prowess earned him the position of admiral in the Mori clan's navy. He faced Oda Nobunaga's fleet in the fierce naval battles at Kizugawaguchi.

Fighting Strength

Luck

Leadership

Humanity

Willpower

Intelligence

Takeyoshi controlled the fleets, politics, and shipping in the Seto Inland Sea.

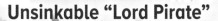

Unsinkable "Lord Pirate"
KUKI YOSHITAKA

九鬼嘉隆

Born: 1542
Died: 1600
Died at age 59 by his own hand

Fighting Strength

Luck

Leadership

Humanity

Willpower

Intelligence

Nobunaga ordered Yoshitaka to do the impossible: build a fireproof warship. He succeeded and became known as "Lord Pirate."

After proving his worth among the pirates of Shima Province, Kuki Yoshitaka was appointed by Oda Nobunaga to be the admiral of his fleet. But the armada of the Mori clan proved overwhelming at the first Battle of Kizugawaguchi. To get his revenge, Yoshitaka built an ironclad warship that was like a floating metal castle. At the second Battle of Kizugawaguchi, his flagship obliterated the Mori fleet.

1
Oda
Clan

2
Takeda, Uesugi,
and Hojo Clans

3
Toyotomi
Clan

4
Mori
Clan

5
Date
Clan

6
Shimazu, Otomo,
and Chosokabe
Clans

7
Tokugawa
Clan

8
Other
Samurai

Stood His Ground
KENNYO

顕如

Born: 1543
Died: 1592
Died at
age 50
from illness

Kennyo was a Buddhist monk of the Pure Land sect's head temple in Kyoto. He saw Oda Nobunaga as an enemy to Buddhism and vowed to stop him. Through an alliance with the Azai, Asakura, and Takeda clans (and with the help of the reigning shogun Ashikaga Yoshiaki) Kennyo formed a net of enemies around Nobunaga's forces that kept him tied up in battle for about 10 years.

Fighting
Strength

Luck

Leadership

Humanity

Willpower

Intelligence

Kennyo used all his strength to stubbornly resist Nobunaga's bid to unify the nation by force.

36

The Ultimate Betrayal
AKECHI MITSUHIDE

Born: 1528 (?)
Died: 1582 (?)
Died at age 55 (?)
in battle

明
智
光
秀

Akechi Mitsuhide was one of Oda Nobunaga's "Four Heavenly Kings."

While Nobunaga slept at Honnoji Temple, Mitsuhide struck. He wanted to be shogun of all Japan, but just 11 days later, Toyotomi Hideyoshi come to avenge their master. Mitsuhide's army was scattered, and the great warrior Mitsuhide was stabbed to death by farmers wielding bamboo spears.

Fighting Strength

Luck

Leadership

Humanity

Willpower

Intelligence

Clever and ambitious enough to topple Nobunaga, Mitsuhide fell soon after betraying his master.

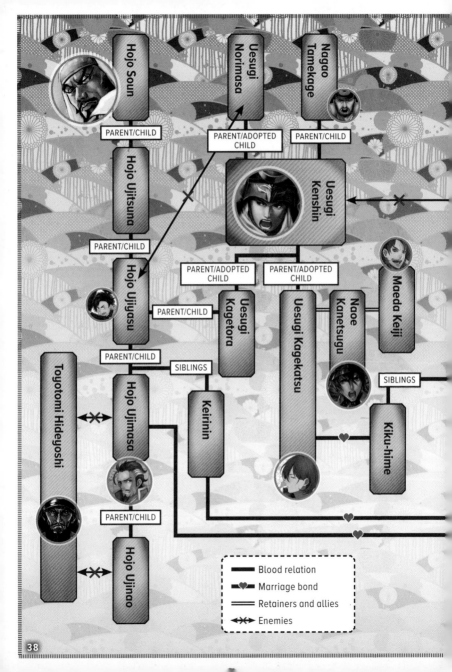

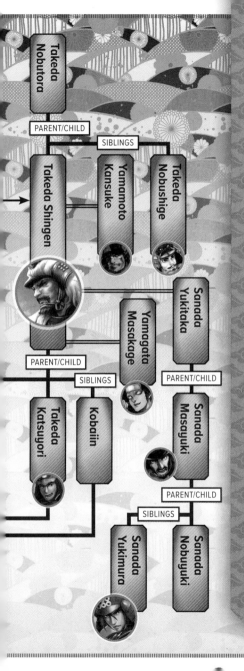

CHAPTER 2

THE TAKEDA CLAN

THE UESUGI CLAN

THE HOJO CLAN

AND THEIR RELATIONS

These three clans controlled central and eastern Japan, making alliances one day and going for the jugular the next.

The Tiger Who Rode Under Nature's Banner

TAKEDA SHINGEN

Born: 1521
Died: 1573
Died at age 53 from illness
Birthplace: Kai Province (present-day Yamanashi Prefecture)
Father: Takeda Nobutora
Son: Takeda Katsuyori

Main Base

🏯 Tsutsujigasaki Castle (Yamanashi)

"Swift as the wind, quiet as the forest, aggressive as an inferno, unmoving as a mountain." These are the words written on the battle standards of Takeda Shingen, the Tiger of Kai Province.

As a young man, Shingen rebelled against the selfish ways his father ruled his people. When he took control of the clan, he improved Kai Province. He reformed the legal code, developed new farmland, and improved irrigation.

Five times Shingen met his rival Uesugi Kenshin on the battlefield of Kawanakajima—without a clear winner being decided. Still, Shingen's territory expanded and, in 1572, he set off for Kyoto to follow his dream of unifying the country.

At the Battle of Mikatagahara, Shingen smashed the armies of Tokugawa Ieyasu. He allied his forces with the Azai and Asakura clans and the monks of Ishiyama Honganji Temple. But the next year, Shingen fell—not to an enemy, but to a disease. He warned: "If our enemies learn of my death, they will attack our clan. Keep my death a secret for at least three years." These were the Tiger's last words.

疾如風
徐如林
侵掠如火
不動如山

40

武田信玄
たけ だ しん げん

Fighting
Strength

Luck

Leadership

Humanity

Willpower

Intelligence

Shingen was a mighty warrior feared by the
local lords yet beloved by his own people.

The Dragon of Echigo
UESUGI KENSHIN

Born: 1530
Died: 1578
Died at age 49 from illness
Birthplace: Echigo Province (present-day Niigata Prefecture)
Father: Nagao Tamekage
Adopted Son: Uesugi Kagekatsu

Main Base
Kasugayama Castle (Niigata)

Uesugi Kenshin was such a fierce warrior that he earned himself two nicknames on the field of battle: "The Dragon of Echigo" and "God of War."

Kenshin was known to be compassionate, and he often came to the rescue of lords fleeing from defeat. Kenshin soon earned the animosity of the warriors Takeda Shingen and Hojo Ujiyasu by harboring their defeated enemies. He faced his rivals at the Battle of Kawanakajima. Over and over, their armies clashed. But in the end, it was Kenshin's brainpower that won the day. He saw through the strategies of Yamamoto Kansuke, Shingen's top strategic adviser, and, in their fourth battle, he emerged victorious.

Sending Salt to Your Enemy

In Japanese there's a saying "sending salt to your enemy." No, it doesn't mean rubbing salt in someone's wounds. In fact, it means just the opposite: showing compassion when you have the advantage. And it comes from the life of Uesugi Kenshin.

In the midst of all the warring among clans, Kenshin learned that the rival Takeda clan was suffering because the Imagawa clan had cut off their supply routes. The Takeda domain was landlocked, so they did not have access to the sea salt they needed to survive. Rather than take advantage of his weakened enemy, Kenshin sent Takeda Shingen a shipment of salt. His act of compassion lives on in language and history.

42

Kenshin went on to defeat the army of Oda Nobunaga's retainer Shibata Katsuie at the Battle of Tedori River. After the victory, he told his own retainers that the throne of the shogun was within their grasp. Sadly, the next year, he fell ill and died.

上杉謙信

Fighting Strength

Luck

Leadership

Humanity

Willpower

Intelligence

Kenshin was a heroic warrior who filled his heart with compassion and culture.

43

A Free-Spirited Bohemian
MAEDA KEIJI

Born: ?
Died: ?
Cause of death unknown

前田慶次

As a young man, Maeda Keiji went to Kyoto to study literature. His lifestyle earned him the name "Kabukimono," which means "flamboyant, eccentric person." When he returned to the clan, he became close with Naoe Kanetsugu, who secured him a position fighting for the Uesugi clan. After their loss at the Battle of Sekigahara, Keiji stopped Kanetsugu from taking his own life.

Fighting Strength

Luck

Leadership

Humanity

Willpower

Intelligence

Keiji loved reading and was an expert with a sword.

44

A Dignified Leader
UESUGI KAGEKATSU

Born: 1555
Died: 1623
Died at age 69 from illness

上杉景勝

The adopted son of Uesugi Kenshin, Uesugi Kagekatsu rarely showed his emotions, but he cared for his people and ruled fairly. When Toyotomi Hideyoshi emerged as the most powerful lord in the land, Kagekatsu chose to follow him. On Hideyoshi's death, however, a fight for the throne ensued. Kagekatsu squared off against Tokugawa Ieyasu at the Battle of Sekigahara, where Ieyasu proved victorious. Afterward, Kagekatsu became one of his retainers.

Fighting Strength

Luck

Leadership

Humanity

Willpower

Intelligence

Quiet and dignified, Kagekatsu sat on Hideyoshi's trusted Council of Elders.

A Loyal Friend and Benevolent Leader
NAOE KANETSUGU

Born: 1560
Died: 1619
Died at age 60 from illness
Birthplace: Echigo Province (present-day Niigata Prefecture)
Father: Higuchi Kanetoyo
Wife: Osen (daughter of Naoe Kagetsuna)

Main Base

Yonezawa Castle (Yamagata)

When he was a boy, Naoe Kanetsugu became one of Uesugi Kenshin's samurai. After Kenshin's death, he went on to serve Kenshin's son Uesugi Kagekatsu. The two forged a deep friendship.

When Kagekatsu joined forces with Toyotomi Hideyoshi, Kanetsugu followed his master's lead, and a lifelong rivalry with Hideyoshi's chief opponent—Tokugawa Ieyasu—was born! Kanetsugu even sent a letter of challenge to the powerful lord, which fanned the flames of the great Battle of Sekigahara.

As commanders in the western army, Kagekatsu and Kanetsugu rode together to fight against the eastern army's Date Masamune and Mogami Yoshiaki. Eventually Ieyasu's armies won the day, and both Kagekatsu and Kanetsugu bent their knees to the new shogun. As punishment for their years of resistance, Ieyasu greatly decreased their holdings. But even in his smaller domain of Yonezawa, Kanetsugu still took care of his own retainers and common folk. He devoted his later years to educating his people.

直江兼続
なおえかねつぐ

Fighting Strength

Luck

Leadership

Humanity

Willpower

Intelligence

Kanetsugu excelled at scholarship and martial arts, and never flinched before authority.

47

Firearms Enter Japan!

These new weapons came from Europe.
How did samurai use them?

Shimazu Takahisa

The first firearms to enter Japan were matchlock muskets imported through Tanegashima Island. The samurai in charge of the island was named Tanegashima Tokitaka, and he started replicating the guns. Shimazu Takahisa from the Satsuma clan was among the first samurai to use firearms in battle. Soon firearms had spread throughout the land.

Takahisa was the first general to get his hands on the fearsome new weapons.

Oda Nobunaga

Japan's Original Musketeers

Saika Magoichi

After suffering at the hands of the Saika mercenaries who were early adopters of firearms, Oda Nobunaga formed a battalion of 3,000 musketeers (soldiers trained to use the guns) and led them to defeat Takeda Katsuyori and others.

Even today, Wakayama Prefecture is famous for its gunsmiths. This long history began with Saika Magoichi, leader of the Saika mercenaries, who made thousands of muskets to use against Nobunaga and the forces of unification.

Soldiers without muskets attacked on foot and horseback.

Soldiers used platforms for scouting the enemy and shouting out orders.

Fences with high wooden stakes (called palisades) were built to keep out enemy soldiers and horses.

Musketeers arranged themselves in long, thin formations to fire on their attackers from many angles.

The Three Musketeers? Try 3,000!

49

The Guardian of the Toyotomi Clan
SANADA YUKIMURA

Born: 1567
Died: 1615
Died at age 49 in battle
Birthplace: Shinano Province (present-day Nagano Prefecture)
Father: Sanada Masayuki
Elder Brother: Sanada Nobuyuki

Main Base

Ueda Castle (Nagano)

Sanada Yukimura, also known by his real name Sanada Nobushige, served the Toyotomi clan along with his father, Sanada Masayuki. He fought to repel Tokugawa Ieyasu.

After the Battle of Sekigahara, as the conflict between Ieyasu and the Toyotomi clan worsened, Yukimura joined the force defending Osaka Castle. During the winter campaign of the Siege of Osaka, Yukimura built the famous Sanadamaru, an indestructible fortification. He also came up with an excellent strategy using troops armed with muskets. And he successfully held off the army of Ieyasu, which was 200,000 strong!

Amazed by his defeat, Ieyasu invited Yukimura to join his army, promising to give him Shinano Province. Yukimura rejected the offer. During the summer campaign the following year, Yukimura charged the enemy headquarters, aiming to take Ieyasu's head. He came close, but was killed before reaching Ieyasu.

真田幸村

Fighting
Strength

Luck

Leadership

Humanity

Willpower

Intelligence

Yukimura's toughness and courage were praised by
friends and foes alike. Even today he is referred to
as "Sanada, the best warrior of Japan."

1	2	3	4	5	6	7	8
Oda Clan	Takeda, Uesugi, and Hojo Clans	Toyotomi Clan	Mori Clan	Date Clan	Shimazu, Otomo, and Chosokabe Clans	Tokugawa Clan	Other Samurai

The First Feudal Lord of the Warring States Period

HOJO SOUN

Born: 1432
Died: 1519
Died at age 88 from illness
Birthplace: Bicchu Province (present-day Okayama Prefecture)
Son: Hojo Ujitsuna
Grandson: Hojo Ujiyasu

Main Base

Odawara Castle (Kanagawa)

The Warring States period was a time of turmoil and bloodshed when feudal lords fought to enlarge their domains and eventually seize the nation's throne. The era began when the shoguns living in Muromachi could no longer prevent their retainer lords from fighting. The lord who kicked off the battle was Hojo Soun.

But Soun's first move was not a violent one. His younger sister had married into the Imagawa clan. The clan was being torn apart by a vicious struggle over who would succeed to the lordship, so Soun stepped in and brokered a peaceful solution. As a reward, he was granted command of Kokokuji Castle. From there, Soun used a mix of politics and force to slowly expand the domains under his control.

Another battle for succession (and there were many) was raging in neighboring Izu Province. This time, Soun didn't wait to negotiate—he went in and took the territory by force from the squabbling heirs. Once in Izu, the strongholds of Odawara and Misaki Castles soon fell to him before he turned east and gobbled up all of Sagamino Province. When he was not on the battlefield, he was a shrewd politician, beloved by the people in the territories he controlled.

北条早雲

Soun's Secret Weapon: Fire Cattle

To capture Odawara Castle, Soun ordered his men to drive 1,000 cattle onto Mt. Hakone at night. He then had them tie torches to the cattle's horns before driving them around the mountain in circles. The defenders of the castle looked up at the mountain and thought a huge army was descending on them. They were thrown into a panic, and Soun easily stormed the castle and took it for himself.

Fighting Strength

Luck

Leadership

Humanity

Willpower

Intelligence

Soun was a master strategist in battle and politics who always had an ace up his sleeve.

Undefeated Warrior and Scholar
HOJO UJIYASU

**Born: 1515
Died: 1571
Died at age 57 from illness**

Hojo Ujiyasu was the grandson of Hojo Soun. He is remembered for leading a daring surprise nighttime attack known as the Kawagoe Night Battle, when he routed forces of the Uesugi clan who had surrounded Kawagoe Castle. Ujiyasu's victory made him the ruler of much of the Kanto region. To shore up control, he made careful alliances with the Takeda and Imagawa clans.

北条氏康

Fighting Strength

Luck

Leadership

Humanity

Willpower

Intelligence

Ujiyasu was the perfect leader: a fierce fighter, a calm strategist, and a skillful negotiator.

An Unthinkable Surrender

HOJO UJIMASA

Born: 1538
Died: 1590
Died at age 53 by his own hand

北条氏政

Fighting Strength

Luck

Leadership

Humanity

Willpower

Intelligence

Ujimasa expanded the clan's domain to its peak but could not hold on.

From his home base at Odawara, Hojo Ujimasa (son of Hojo Ujiyasu) ruled over the Kanto region. Toyotomi Hideyoshi, who ruled over western Japan, demanded Ujimasa's allegiance. Ujimasa refused, thus inviting the Seige of Odawara. Hideyoshi mobilized an enormous army to surround his rival. Ujimasa surrendered and committed *seppuku* (ritual suicide), bringing his life—and the 100-year reign of the Hojo clan—to an end.

Look Your Best and Protect Your Chest

Tricked-Out Samurai Armor

Maedate

Decoration on the front of the helmet

Menbo

Covering that protects the face

Wakidate

Decoration on the side of the helmet

Nodowa

Gorget, which protects the throat

Fukikaeshi

Deflects swords and arrows from the face

Osode

Shoulder and arm protection

Do

Chest and stomach protection

Chosokabe Nobuchika

His helmet is made out of leather. The *maedate* is in the shape of a dragon, and the *wakidate* are stag's antlers.

Kusazuri

Protects the lower body

Collection of the Sekkeiji Temple

Kato Kiyomasa

The rings on the *fukikaeshi* and *do* represent snake eyes, the family crest of the Kato clan. They are decorated with real gold leaf. The tall, pointed top of the helmet is made with layers upon layers of ultra-thin Japanese paper pressed together.

Naoe Kanetsugu

This famous armor is known for the Chinese character that adorns the helmet. It means "love." It is the first character in the name of Aizen Myoo, a ferocious red-skinned Buddhist god of rage and passion.

Date Masamune

The part of this armor that covered the fighter's torso is made up of five black-lacquered pieces. The crescent moon shape on the helmet is gold-plated.

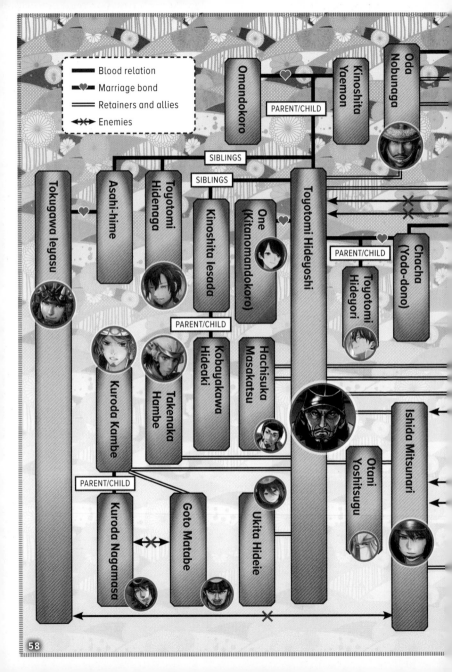

Legend:
- Blood relation
- ♥ Marriage bond
- Retainers and allies
- ◆✕◆ Enemies

Oda Nobunaga

Kinoshita Yaemon

Omandokoro

PARENT/CHILD

SIBLINGS

SIBLINGS

Tokugawa Ieyasu

Asahi-hime

Toyotomi Hidenaga

Kinoshita Iesada

One (Kitanomandokoro)

Toyotomi Hideyoshi

Chacha (Yodo-dono)

PARENT/CHILD

Toyotomi Hideyori

PARENT/CHILD

Kuroda Kambe

Takenaka Hambe

Kobayakawa Hideaki

Hachisuka Masakatsu

Ishida Mitsunari

Otani Yoshitsugu

PARENT/CHILD

Kuroda Nagamasa

◆✕◆

Goto Matabe

Ukita Hideie

✕

58

CHAPTER 3

THE TOYOTOMI CLAN

AND THEIR RELATIONS

Stepping into Oda Nobunaga's shoes, this clan united the nation. The momentum of their success swept away their enemies, but also bred new ones from inside their own ranks: Ishida Mitsunari would have his own say in who sat on the throne.

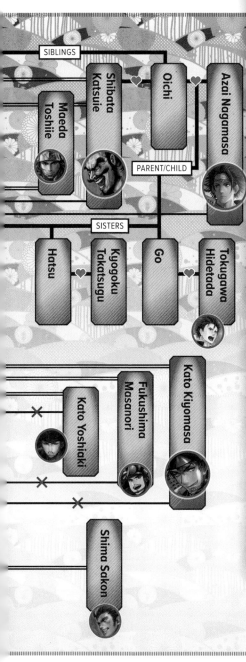

SIBLINGS

Maeda Toshie

Shibata Katsuie

Oichi

Azai Nagamasa

PARENT/CHILD

SISTERS

Hatsu

Kyogoku Takatsugu

Go

Tokugawa Hidetada

Kato Yoshiaki

Fukushima Masanori

Kato Kiyomasa

Shima Sakon

Map of Feudal Japan
1580
HIDEYOSHI
on the Road to Victory!

**Ryuzoji
Takanobu**

**Mori
Terumoto**

**Oda
Nobunaga**

**Tachibana
Muneshige**

**Otomo
Sorin**

Oki

Mori Clan

Tsushima

Iki

Ryuzoji Clan

Izumo Hoki Inaba Tang

Iwami Shimane Tottori Tajima

Nagato Aki Bingo Bicchu Mimasaka Harima Kyot

Yamaguchi Hiroshima Okayama Bizen Hyogo Ta

Suo Bizen Sette

Chikuzen Sanuki Kagawa Awaji Osak

Fukuoka Buzen Kav

Saga Iyo Awa Izumi

Chikugo Ehime Tosa Tokushima

Hizen Oita Kochi Kii

Nagasaki Bungo Wakay

Otomo
Clan

Higo Chosokabe Clan

Kumamoto

Miyazaki

Kagoshima Hyuga

Satsuma

Osumi Shimazu
Clan

**Shimazu
Yoshihisa**

**Chosokabe
Motochika**

60

Oda Nobunaga started down the long road to the throne, but in 1582 that road ended with his betrayal at Honnoji Temple. His successor, Toyotomi Hideyoshi, took up the task where his lord left off.

Aomori

Dewa
Akita

Mutsu
Iwate

Uesugi
Kagekatsu

Sado

Yamagata
Miyagi

Uesugi
Clan

Echigo
Niigata

Fukushima

Noto

Kaga Toyama
Etchu

Kozuke
Gunma

Shimotsuke
Tochigi

Date
Clan

Date
Masamune

Fukui
Echizen
Ishikawa
Hida

Shinano

Hitachi

Oda Clan

Nagano
Mino

Shiga
Gifu
Owari

Kai

Saitama
Musashi
Ibaraki

Omi
Aichi
Mikawa

Yamanashi
Sagami
Tokyo

Shimousa

Ise
Shizuoka
Suruga

Kanagawa
Kazusa

Hojo
Ujimasa

Mie
Totomi
Izu

Chiba

Shima

Tokugawa
Clan

Awa

Hojo Clan

Tokugawa
Ieyasu

KEY

Old border

------- Current prefectural border

Owari Old province names are black.

Aichi Present-day prefecture names are white.

61

The Man Who United a Nation

TOYOTOMI HIDEYOSHI

Born: 1537
Died: 1598
Died at age 62
from illness
Birthplace:
Owari Province
(present-day Aichi
Prefecture)
Wife: One
(Kitanomandokoro),
Yodo-dono
Son: Toyotomi
Hideyori

Main Base

Osaka Castle
(Osaka)

Toyotomi Hideyoshi was always on the lookout for ways of winning without warfare. In this manner, he united all the warring states under one banner.

Originally named Hashiba Hideyoshi, he was born into a poor farming family. As a young man, he ran away to become a warrior. First Hideyoshi had to find a powerful lord to serve as a samurai. He joined the service of the man who was expected to become the unifier of the country—Oda Nobunaga.

Over countless battles Hideyoshi proved his skill and intelligence. He started moving up in the world. When Nobunaga was betrayed by Akechi Mitsuhide, in the midst of the war with the Mori clan, Hideyoshi rode out immediately and arrived before any other retainer to avenge his master.

After Nobunaga's untimely death, Hideyoshi became the head of the Oda clan. He fought to unify every corner of the land under his banners. At last, in 1590, Hideyoshi completed the dream of unification. He was made chief adviser to the Emperor, who gave him the new name "Toyotomi."

Winning Nobunaga's Favor—with Warm Slippers

How did the son of a poor farmer gain the favor of one of the most powerful lords in the nation? Hideyoshi knew he needed to stand out from the other servants. So during the winter, Hideyoshi put Nobunaga's slippers inside his clothes to keep them warm. In the morning, Nobunaga had warm slippers—and a growing admiration for the thoughtfulness of his young servant.

豊臣秀吉
とよ とみ ひで よし

Fighting Strength

Luck

Leadership

Humanity

Willpower

Intelligence

Hideyoshi convinced his enemies to become his allies and quickly united the nation.

Hideyoshi's Right-Hand Man
KURODA KAMBE

Born: 1546
Died: 1604
Died at age 59 from illness
Birthplace: Harima Province (present-day Hyogo Prefecture)
Father: Kuroda Mototaka
Son: Kuroda Nagamasa

Main Base

Himeji Castle (Hyogo)

Kuroda Kambe's career did not get off to the most auspicious start. As a servant of Oda Nobunaga, Kambe was sent to negotiate with Araki Murashige, a rebellious retainer. The negotiations went sour, and the next thing he knew, Kambe found himself thrown in jail! He was eventually rescued, but his left leg was badly injured in the escape. From then on, he was carried out to battle on a platform.

Nobunaga ordered Kambe to join his young retainer Toyotomi Hideyoshi as a councillor, and the two set off on an illustrious string of victories. From the siege of Tottori Castle to the amphibious assault on Bicchu Takamatsu Castle, Kambe was responsible for many of the era's most famous battle plans.

After the betrayal at Honnoji Temple, Kambe urged Hideyoshi to break off his conflict with the Mori clan and consolidate his troops from the front lines. This proved to be the perfect tactical decision and paved the way for Hideyoshi to eventually emerge victorious from all other factions. Kambe later changed his name to Josui (which means "like water") and vowed to serve Hideyoshi for the rest of his life with a heart as clear as water.

黒田官兵衛

Fighting
Strength

Luck

Leadership

Humanity

Willpower

Intelligence

Kambe served first Nobunaga and then Hideyoshi as
their most trusted adviser in countless battles.

A Master Tactician
TAKENAKA HAMBE

Born: 1544
Died: 1579

Died at age 36 from illness

Birthplace: Mino Province (present-day Gifu Prefecture)

Father: Takenaka Shigemoto

Son: Takenaka Shigekado

Main Base

Bodaisan Castle (Gifu)

Takenaka Hambe's real name was Takenaka Shigeharu. His first job was as a retainer of Saito Tatsuoki. But Tatsuoki cared more about his own pleasure than leading his clan and paid no heed to Hambe's advice and warnings. One day, Hambe—with only 16 loyal followers—stormed Tatsuoki's castle and took it for his own.

Having made his point, Hambe returned the castle to Tatsuoki. But the demonstration attracted the notice of Oda Nobunaga, who sent Toyotomi Hideyoshi to ask Hambe to become a retainer of the Oda clan. Hambe refused, but eventually Hideyoshi's passion and persistence won out. Hambe agreed to serve the clan, but only as one of Hideyoshi's samurai.

Soon Hambe proved his genius for military tactics in Hideyoshi's army. He was especially good at convincing his enemies to surrender with a minimum of casualties.

Hambe had a brilliant career as a warrior and politician ahead of him. Unfortunately, when he was only 36 years old, he became ill during the Battle of Miki Castle and died in camp.

竹中半兵衛

Fighting
Strength

Luck

Leadership

Humanity

Willpower

Intelligence

Hambe's perfect blend of wisdom and
courage served Hideyoshi well.

The Spear King
MAEDA TOSHIIE

Born: 1538
Died: 1599
Died at age 62 from illness
Birthplace: Owari Province (present-day Aichi Prefecture)
Father: Maeda Toshiharu
Wife: Matsu

Main Base

Kanazawa Castle (Ishikawa)

Maeda Toshiie made the most of his friendship with Toyotomi Hideyoshi and helped him to unify the nation.

From a young age, Toshiie served Oda Nobunaga alongside Hideyoshi. They were neighbors, so they grew up like brothers.

After the betrayal at Honnoji Temple, the struggle for leadership of the clan led Hideyoshi to fight against his fellow retainer Shibata Katsuie at the Battle of Shizugatake. At the time of the battle, Toshiie was still one of Katsuie's subordinate officers. This conflict of interest put him in a terrible position. In the end, he decided he could not turn his spear against his best friend. Miraculously, the fearsome Katsuie understood Toshiie's plight and accepted his decision.

Toshiie continued to serve and advise at Hideyoshi's side. Hideyoshi trusted him so much that when he became sick and knew he was on the verge of death, he entrusted Toshiie with the life of his son Hideyori. Unfortunately, Toshiie succumbed to disease exactly one year later, and was unable to defend Hideyori against Tokugawa Ieyasu's ambition.

前田利家

Fighting Strength

Luck

Leadership

Humanity

Willpower

Intelligence

A big man with a bigger heart, Toshiie was a defender of the Oda and Toyotomi clans.

69

Lifelong Protector of Hideyoshi
HACHISUKA MASAKATSU

Born: 1526
Died: 1586
Died at age 61 from illness

蜂須賀正勝

According to rumors, Hachisuka Masakatsu was once the kingpin of a band of highway robbers. He fought in many of the major encounters in Toyotomi Hideyoshi's rise to power, including the assault on the Azai and Asakura clans; the stormings of the Miki, Tottori, and Bicchu Takamatsu Castles; and the Battle of Komaki and Nagakute. Masakatsu served Hideyoshi faithfully until the end of his life.

Fighting Strength

Luck

Leadership

Humanity

Willpower

Intelligence

Masakatsu was equally skilled in battle and at the negotiating table.

TOYOTOMI HIDENAGA

Born: 1540
Died: 1591
Died at age 52 from illness

豊臣秀長

Toyotomi Hidenaga was three years younger than Toyotomi Hideyoshi, and they were very close. When Hideyoshi went to serve Oda Nobunaga, Hidenaga followed. After Nobunaga's death, Hidenaga helped his brother unify the nation—making the most of his calm disposition to play the diplomat among the always-vying retainers, who trusted his good judgment.

Fighting Strength

Luck

Leadership

Humanity

Willpower

Intelligence

Skilled in not only military matters but in politics and administration, Hidenaga earned the deep trust of the clan's retainers.

71

Legendary Samurai Showdowns

Here are three battles that changed the course of Japan's history.

The Battle of Okehazama

Imagawa Yoshimoto was camped at Okehazama with a massive force of 25,000 soldiers when Oda Nobunaga led a surprise attack. Nobunaga and his 3,000 hand-picked men won the day!

Winner!

Oda Nobunaga

VS.

Imagawa Yoshimoto

Marching Through the Storm

KEY POINT

Nobunaga rose from his sleeping roll before dawn. He gulped down a bowl of porridge while standing up and giving orders. The troops set out in the middle of a raging thunderstorm. The rain was so heavy they couldn't see the soldier marching ahead of them, but still Nobunaga urged them on. He knew the rain was their protection, the key to their victory. It allowed them to approach Yoshimoto's army undetected . . . and then they struck.

Okehazama

September 1561

The Battle of Kawanakajima

In another famous encounter, the two master tacticians Takeda Shingen and Uesugi Kenshin met at Mt. Saijo. Shingen split off part of his forces to create a flying column that would attack the Uesugi troops from the rear. But Kenshin was expecting this maneuver! He sent his troops silently down the mountain for their own surprise attack on the Takeda clan's soldiers. The fighting was intense. At the end of the day, both armies accepted a stalemate.

Draw!

Uesugi Kenshin

VS.

Takeda Shingen

The Battle of Shizugatake

Winner!

Toyotomi Hideyoshi

VS.

Shibata Katsuie

Toyotomi Hideyoshi and Shibata Katsuie clashed over who would succeed Nobunaga as the leader of the Oda clan at the Battle of Shizugatake. The two generals had assembled their armies when news came that Oda Nobutaka, third son of Nobunaga, had started his own campaign to control the clan. Hideyoshi decided that Nobutaka was the bigger threat and started to withdraw the main part of his army. Katsuie's retainer Sakuma Morimasa saw his opportunity and attacked the remaining troops. But messengers raced through the night to get word to Hideyoshi, who immediately turned around and smashed the opportunistic attackers at his rear.

Shizugatake

Hideyoshi's Speed

KEY POINT

Hideyoshi's troops had already marched 30 miles away by the time word reached him that Sakuma Morimasa was attacking. He immediately turned his troops around and joined the battle in less than six hours. When they saw the unexpected reinforcements arrive, Morimasa's troops lost their will to fight.

Kawanakajima

The Agile Flying Column

KEY POINT

Shingen's flying column summited Mt. Saijo, only to find that their enemy had disappeared! Fortunately for the Takeda clan, the detachment was able to think and move quickly enough to find the main force again and catch the Uesugi army in a pincer attack, turning what might have been a crushing defeat into a stalemate.

1	2	3	4	5	6	7	8
Oda Clan	Takeda, Uesugi, and Hojo Clans	Toyotomi Clan	Mori Clan	Date Clan	Shimazu, Otomo, and Chosokabe Clans	Tokugawa Clan	Other Samurai

Guardian of the Toyotomi Clan's Prosperity

ISHIDA MITSUNARI

Born: 1560
Died: 1600
Executed at age 41

石田三成

Ishida Mitsunari served as a samurai of the Toyotomi clan. Mitsunari made himself valuable through his military prowess, diplomacy, reconnaissance, and negotiation skills. When Toyotomi Hideyoshi died, Mitsunari vowed to thwart Tokugawa Ieyasu from rising to power. He formed the western army to fight at the decisive Battle of Sekigahara, where he was defeated. Ieyasu had him executed after the battle.

Fighting Strength

Luck

Leadership

Humanity

Willpower

Intelligence

Mitsunari used his shrewd mind for logistics to command armies.

Loyal Friend to the End
OTANI YOSHITSUGU

Born: 1559
Died: 1600
Died at age 42 by his own hand

大谷吉継

As a young man, Otani Yoshitsugu contracted a disfiguring skin disease. Despite this, Ishida Mitsunari never let their friendship wane. After Toyotomi Hideyoshi's death, Mitsunari was determined to go after Tokugawa Ieyasu and fight for the Toyotomi clan. Even though he knew it would mean his own death, Yoshitsugu would not abandon his friend. He joined Mitsunari in the Battle of Sekigahara. When the last of his fighting strength had been drained, Yoshitsugu took his own life.

Fighting Strength

Luck

Leadership

Humanity

Willpower

Intelligence

Yoshitsugu had been a loyal samurai of Hideyoshi since boyhood, mastering politics and government along the way.

75

Ishida Mitsunari's Fighting Partner—and Friend
SHIMA SAKON

Born: 1540
Died: 1600
Died at age 61 in battle
Birthplace: Yamato Province (present-day Nara Prefecture)
Father: Shima Masakatsu
Son: Shima Nobukatsu

Main Base

Tsubai Castle (Nara)

After proving himself to be one of the strongest warriors in the land, Shima Sakon agreed to serve as a samurai of Ishida Mitsunari—who was 20 years younger than him!

Sakon's story is closely tied to Mitsunari's. Mitsunari was a brilliant tactician, but he lacked the physical strength to dominate a battlefield. Sakon was already a famous warrior when Mitsunari approached him with an offer: "I will give you half of my yearly income if you will fight alongside me." If it had been for personal glory, Sakon would not have agreed. But he knew that Mitsunari cared only about protecting and advancing Toyotomi Hideyoshi. This absolute loyalty moved Sakon, and he was persuaded to become Mitsunari's faithful retainer.

Like his new boss, Sakon also had little desire for personal enrichment, and it is said he never collected his half of the income. They developed a relationship of trust and honesty, and people often mistook them for brothers.

At the final showdown at the Battle of Sekigahara, Sakon made a plan with Mitsunari to ambush the Tokugawa headquarters and kill Ieyasu in a suicide attack. They never made it through the vast army that surrounded Ieyasu. But even in the jaws of defeat, Sakon used his body as a shield, buying Mitsunari time to escape back to their camp.

島左近

Fighting Strength

Luck

Leadership

Humanity

Willpower

Intelligence

Sakon was a fierce fighter and clever counselor.

77

1	2	3	4	5	6	7	8
Oda Clan	Takeda, Uesugi, and Hojo Clans	Toyotomi Clan	Mori Clan	Date Clan	Shimazu, Otomo, and Chosokabe Clans	Tokugawa Clan	Other Samurai

Demon with a Spear

KATO KIYOMASA

Born: 1562
Died: 1611

Died at age 50 from illness

Birthplace: Owari Province (present-day Aichi Prefecture)

Father: Kato Kiyotada

Son: Kato Tadahiro

Main Base

Kumamoto Castle (Kumamoto)

Kato Kiyomasa's weapon of choice was the cross-headed spear, and it is rumored he used this type of spear to hunt tigers during the invasion of Korea.

Kiyomasa's mother and Toyotomi Hideyoshi's mother were first cousins. Kiyomasa served Hideyoshi from a young age and became known as a samurai who combined strength and intelligence. He was a favorite of Hideyoshi's wife One.

Kiyomasa held nothing back when he was fighting for Hideyoshi. He cemented his place in his lord's trust at the Battle of Shizugatake, where he was one of the Seven Spears—the seven spearmen who acted as Hideyoshi's personal bodyguards—and made a heroic charge against Shibata Katsuie. He joined in the invasion of the Kyushu region. After that war, he was given Kumamoto Castle to govern.

After Hideyoshi's death, a rift opened in the Toyotomi clan. Kiyomasa had a falling out with Ishida Mitsunari and, in the fateful Battle of Sekigahara, he sided with Tokugawa Ieyasu, tipping the balance in his favor. Kiyomasa still felt dedicated to Hideyoshi's memory and tried to reconcile the Tokugawas with the remaining Toyotomis. Sadly, he died of illness before he could make his dream a reality.

加藤清正

Fighting Strength

Luck

Leadership

Humanity

Willpower

Intelligence

Kiyomasa was a skilled warrior and politician who served Hideyoshi, then switched to Ieyasu's side.

Always Loyal to Hideyoshi

GOTO MATABE

後藤又兵衛

Born: 1560
Died: 1615
Died at age 56 in battle

Goto Matabe's father died when he was very young, and he was raised by Kuroda Kambe. He fought alongside his adopted father many times. But after Toyotomi Hideyoshi's death, he had a falling out with Kambe's son, Nagamasa.

Still loyal to the memory of Hideyoshi, Matabe joined the remaining retainers of the Toyotomi clan during the Siege of Osaka. He fought valiantly to protect the city and the clan, but the Tokugawas were victorious. He died in the same battle that destroyed the clan.

Fighting Strength

Luck

Leadership

Humanity

Willpower

Intelligence

Matabe withdrew his strength from the Kuroda clan that adopted him.

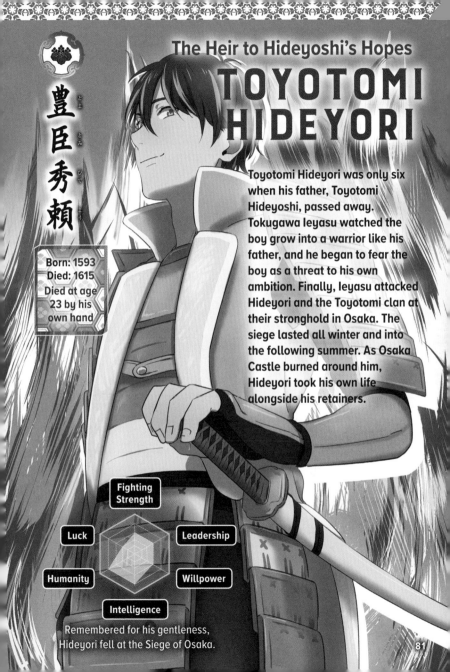

The Heir to Hideyoshi's Hopes
TOYOTOMI HIDEYORI

豊臣秀頼

Born: 1593
Died: 1615
Died at age
23 by his
own hand

Toyotomi Hideyori was only six when his father, Toyotomi Hideyoshi, passed away. Tokugawa Ieyasu watched the boy grow into a warrior like his father, and he began to fear the boy as a threat to his own ambition. Finally, Ieyasu attacked Hideyori and the Toyotomi clan at their stronghold in Osaka. The siege lasted all winter and into the following summer. As Osaka Castle burned around him, Hideyori took his own life alongside his retainers.

Fighting Strength

Luck

Leadership

Humanity

Willpower

Intelligence

Remembered for his gentleness, Hideyori fell at the Siege of Osaka.

4 Astonishing Warriors
Check Out These Daring and Brave Fighters!

Tachibana Dosetsu

He Took on a Lightning Bolt?!

Tachibana Dosetsu was struck by lightning when he was around 35 years old. It is said that he survived by cutting down the lightning bolt with his sword.

He was hurt in the attack, but even with a disabled leg, he still commanded battles, riding on a platform carried by servants. He was known as the "Lightning God."

Kato Kiyomasa

He Battled a Tiger?!

Kato Kiyomasa was incredibly tall and known for his skill with a cross-shaped spear. Legend has it that during the invasion of Korea he came across a tiger. After a fierce battle that left him with only half a spear, he still managed to defeat the tiger!

Shima Sakon   A Ferocious Fighter!

Shima Sakon fought with the western army in the Battle of Sekigahara. When it began to look like the western army would lose the war, he did not give up. In fact, he became even more fierce. He was so terrifying to watch in battle that the warriors of the eastern army were afraid to even look at him. In the last moments of his life, he used his own body as a shield to protect his master, Ishida Mitsunari, and help him get away.

Shimazu Yoshihiro   A Daring Escape!

A courageous warrior, Shimazu Yoshihiro was called "Demon Shimazu." Once, he ended up in a desperate situation: Surrounded by enemies during the Battle of Sekigahara, he tried to kill himself with his sword. At that moment, he heard his nephew's voice saying, "Here in your hometown, the people are looking forward to our lord's safe return." Those words inspired him to fight on. He broke through the enemy lines and returned safely to his home in Satsuma Province.

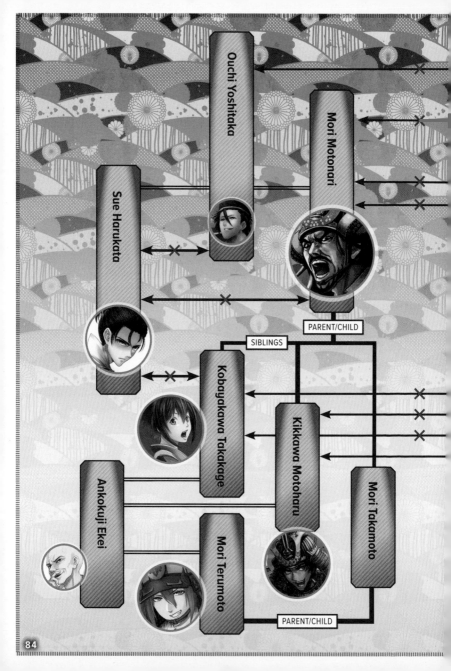

Ouchi Yoshitaka

Mori Motonari

Sue Harukata

PARENT/CHILD

SIBLINGS

Kobayakawa Takakage

Kikkawa Motoharu

Mori Takamoto

Ankokuji Ekei

Mori Terumoto

PARENT/CHILD

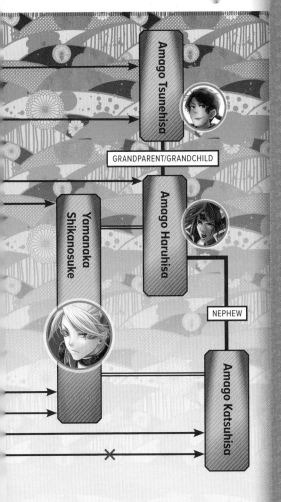

GRANDPARENT/GRANDCHILD

Amago Tsunehisa

Yamanaka Shikanosuke

Amago Haruhisa

NEPHEW

Amago Katsuhisa

Blood relation
Marriage bond
Retainers and allies
Enemies

CHAPTER 4

THE MORI CLAN

AND THEIR RELATIONS

After conquering the powerful Amago and Ouchi clans, the path was clear for Mori Motonari and his three sons to rule over the Chugoku region.

A Fearless Tactician

MORI MOTONARI

Born: 1497
Died: 1571

Died at age 75 from illness

Birthplace: Aki Province (present-day Hiroshima Prefecture)

Sons: Mori Takamoto, Kikkawa Motoharu*, Kobayakawa Takakage*

*sons who married into larger clans and took their brides' family names as their own

Main Base

Yoshida Koriyama Castle (Hiroshima)

Mori Motonari used a combination of political maneuvering and surprise attacks to expand his influence until he had unified the Chugoku region under one banner—the banner of the Mori clan.

Motonari successfully defended his lands, especially against invasion by the Amago clan from Izumo Province in the north. With his borders safe for the moment, Motonari went to work arranging politically advantageous marriages for his sons to the powerful Kikkawa and Kobayakawa clans. The marriages led to alliances. And Motonari so skillfully manipulated these alliances that eventually he controlled both clans' domains.

When Sue Harukata betrayed his lord, Ouchi Yoshitaka, Motonari opposed the betrayal and, in a surprise attack at the Battle of Itsukushima, he destroyed Harukata's large army. Motonari then began an 11-year campaign that culminated with the defeat of the rival Amago clan and the unification of the western provinces of Japan.

The Tale of the Three Arrows

Toward the end of his life, Motonari wrote a long letter to his three sons that was about the importance of cooperation. In it, he used the example of an archer's arrows: Take one arrow and bend it over your knee, he said. See how easily it snaps? Now take three arrows together and try to break them. Not so easy, is it? From this letter, the popular Japanese saying "strong as three arrows" was born.

Fighting Strength

Luck

Leadership

Humanity

Willpower

Intelligence

Motonari devoted his brilliant tactics and brave fighting to his one goal: to expand and protect the Mori clan.

Diplomacy Over War
OUCHI YOSHITAKA

Born: 1507
Died: 1551
Died at age 45 by his own hand

Ouchi Yoshitaka was more interested in fine arts than martial arts. He paid little attention to fighting. Instead, he focused on a prosperous trade with the Korean peninsula. This approach did not sit well with Yoshitaka's warlike retainers. A rebellion led by Sue Harukata broke out and, under the intense pressure of the assault, Yoshitaka took his own life.

大内義隆

- Fighting Strength
- Luck
- Leadership
- Humanity
- Willpower
- Intelligence

Yoshitaka's dream of settling disputes through diplomacy, not violence, did not get far in the Warring States period.

Beloved by the Common People

SUE HARUKATA

Born: 1521
Died: 1555
Died at age 35 by his own hand

Sue Harukata was one of Ouchi Yoshitaka's chief retainers. As the clan's top general, he showed his bravery and ferocity when he routed the Amago clan's army. But Yoshitaka's peaceful politics didn't suit Harukata. Harukata betrayed his lord, forcing him to commit seppuku so he could seize control of the Ouchi clan.

This bold move made Harukata an enemy of Mori Motonari, who surprised him at the Battle of Itsukushima. Harukata perished the same way his former lord had: on his own sword.

陶晴賢

Fighting Strength

Luck

Leadership

Humanity

Willpower

Intelligence

Harukata's strength, intelligence, and the support of his people were no match for the Mori clan.

The Undefeated General
KIKKAWA MOTOHARU

Born: 1530
Died: 1586

Died at age 57 from illness

Birthplace: Aki Province (present-day Hiroshima Prefecture)

Father: Mori Motonari

Brothers: Mori Takamoto, Kobayakawa Takakage

Main Base

Hinoyama Castle (Hiroshima)

Out of the 77 battles Kikkawa Motoharu fought in his life, he won 64 of them, and 13 ended in a stalemate—giving him bragging rights as an undefeated general.

Motoharu was Mori Motonari's second son. His first battle came when he was 11 years old. Despite his father's objections, he rode out with the army and fought against the Amago clan.

His father arranged for him to be married into the wealthy Kikkawa family. When Motoharu became the head of that family, he allied their wealth and troops with his father's. In this new role, he led a successful attack against the Amago clan, greatly expanding the territories controlled by the Mori clan.

Motoharu also faced off against Toyotomi Hideyoshi in the famous Siege of Bicchu Takamatsu Castle. After intense fighting, Hideyoshi suddenly asked to negotiate a truce and left the battle to return to Kyoto. When he learned that Hideyoshi's reason for leaving was to avenge Oda Nobunaga's death, Motoharu was furious. Was Nobunaga more important than the men who had died defending the castle? Motoharu planned to follow Hideyoshi to Kyoto to fight him there, but his younger brother stopped him.

Eventually the Mori clan submitted to Hideyoshi's rule, but Motoharu never forgot his grudge. Rather than fight for the Toyotomis, he retired from battle altogether.

Fighting Strength

Luck

Leadership

Humanity

Willpower

Intelligence

吉川元春

Motoharu loved to read and was famous for copying classic literature in his tent.

Another Impressive Brother

KOBAYAKAWA TAKAKAGE

Born: 1533
Died: 1597

Died at age 65 from illness

Birthplace: Aki Province (present-day Hiroshima Prefecture)

Father: Mori Motonari

Brothers: Mori Takamoto, Kikkawa Motoharu

Son: Kobayakawa Hideaki

Main Base

Mihara Castle (Hiroshima)

The third son of Mori Motonari, Kobayakawa Takakage was famous for not only his brains but also his good looks. Along with his brother Motoharu, he became one of the pillars supporting the Mori clan.

Like his older brother, Takakage married into a wealthy family from Aki Province—the Kobayakawa family—and went on to assume complete control of the family's army and assets.

Takakage was eloquent and persuasive. When trouble arose with the pirates of the Seto Inland Sea, instead of trying to fight them, Takakage persuaded their leader, Murakami Takeyoshi, to join his side. As allies, they ruled the seas.

When Toyotomi Hideyoshi suddenly left the Siege of Bicchu Takamatsu Castle to avenge Oda Nobunaga's death, Takakage persuaded his brother not to try to finish the fight in Kyoto. Takakage was perceptive enough to see that Hideyoshi would be the one to unify the nation and that it would be in the clan's best interest to become one of his supporters.

小早川隆景

An Adopted Nephew

Hideyoshi once asked Mori Terumoto (Motonari's grandson) if he would take his nephew in as his adopted son. This was a great honor—except for the fact that his nephew had a terrible reputation as a troublemaker. Always the peacemaker, Takakage stepped in and offered to take the boy under his own wing to prevent the trouble the young man might have stirred inside the Mori family.

Fighting Strength

Luck

Leadership

Humanity

Willpower

Intelligence

In battle and in politics, Takakage's first concern was always to protect the Mori clan.

Commander in Chief of the Western Army
MORI TERUMOTO

Born: 1553
Died: 1625
Died at age 73 from illness

毛利輝元

Mori Terumoto was the son of Mori Motonari's first son, Takamoto. He became a chief retainer of the Toyotomi clan, even sitting on the distinguished Council of Elders. He was then appointed commander in chief of the ill-fated western armies at the Battle of Sekigahara. But in the wake of their defeat, his lands were drastically reduced by the victorious Tokugawas.

Fighting Strength

Luck

Leadership

Humanity

Willpower

Intelligence

Terumoto kept the clan together with the help of powerful uncles, but in the end, his strength was lacking.

94

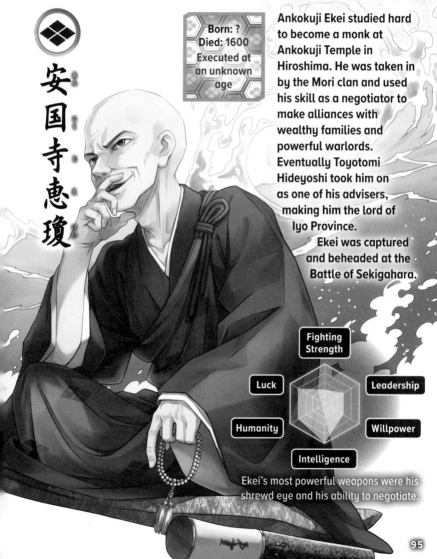

ANKOKUJI EKEI

安国寺恵瓊

Born: ?
Died: 1600
Executed at an unknown age

Ankokuji Ekei studied hard to become a monk at Ankokuji Temple in Hiroshima. He was taken in by the Mori clan and used his skill as a negotiator to make alliances with wealthy families and powerful warlords. Eventually Toyotomi Hideyoshi took him on as one of his advisers, making him the lord of Iyo Province.

Ekei was captured and beheaded at the Battle of Sekigahara.

Fighting Strength

Luck

Leadership

Humanity

Willpower

Intelligence

Ekei's most powerful weapons were his shrewd eye and his ability to negotiate.

95

Leader of the "Mighty Ten"
YAMANAKA SHIKANOSUKE

Born: 1545 (?)
Died: 1578
Murdered at age 34 (?)
Birthplace: Izumo Province (present-day Shimane Prefecture)
Father: Yamanaka Mitsuyuki
Son: Yamanaka Yukimoto

Main Base

Gassan Toda Castle (Shimane)

From a very young age, Yamanaka Shikanosuke served as one of the Amago clan's samurai—that is, until Mori Motonari conquered the clan and took their lands. Later, a band of retainers known as the "Mighty Ten" spearheaded the return of the Amago clan, with Shikanosuke as their leader.

The first step in Shikanosuke's plan was to bring Amago Katsuhisa back from Kyoto (where he was studying to become a Buddhist monk) and make him a soldier. Shikanosuke then prayed to the moon: "If the Amago clan is restored to their rightful lands, then I will gladly undergo the tortures of the seven layers of hell."

The chance came with Toyotomi Hideyoshi's assault on the Mori clan. Hideyoshi entrusted Shikanosuke with an entire flank of his army, and, together with Katsuhisa, they rode out to battle. But the massive power of Kikkawa Motoharu's army was too much for Shikanosuke's troops.

Seeing that his troops could fight no longer, Shikanosuke surrendered. After a tearful farewell, Katsuhisa took his own life, and Shikanosuke was taken prisoner. Shikanosuke hoped he would have one chance to face Motoharu and take his life.

Suspecting this, the Mori clan put him under heavy guard. Even so, Shikanosuke was murdered while being moved from his cell one day, without ever fulfilling his dreams of restoration and revenge.

山中鹿介

Fighting Strength

Luck

Leadership

Humanity

Willpower

Intelligence

An unmatched fighter in one-on-one combat, Shikanosuke was unable to take down the Mori clan.

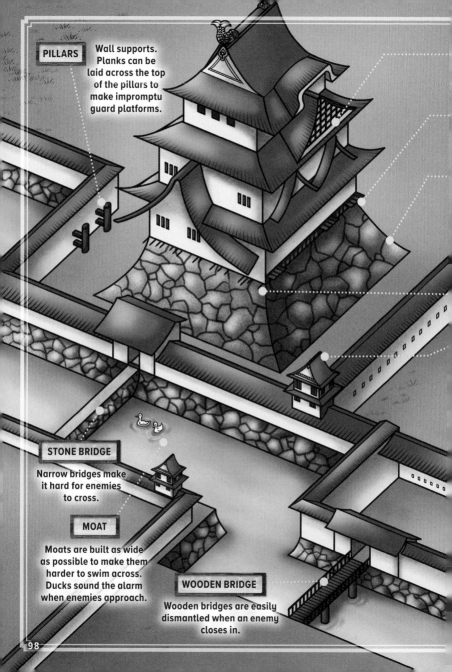

PILLARS Wall supports. Planks can be laid across the top of the pillars to make impromptu guard platforms.

STONE BRIDGE

Narrow bridges make it hard for enemies to cross.

MOAT

Moats are built as wide as possible to make them harder to swim across. Ducks sound the alarm when enemies approach.

WOODEN BRIDGE

Wooden bridges are easily dismantled when an enemy closes in.

Secrets of Famous
CASTLES

INGENIOUS IDEAS TO WIN THE DAY

LATTICEWORK Archers can shoot arrows through the openings in the lattice windows.

MURDER HOLES Openings like these allow castle dwellers to throw rocks or fire muskets and arrows at attackers below.

Walls are curved to make them harder to climb.

ARROW SLITS Archers can fire through the slits.

NINJA DEFLECTORS Spikes on the walls prevent enemies from climbing over.

TURRETS Watchtowers allow people to keep an eye on who or what is approaching the castle.

Walls built near gates keep the enemy from running in a straight line, buying time for people inside the castle to counterattack.

Japanese castles are full of tricks, traps, and surprises to fend off enemy attacks.

GATE

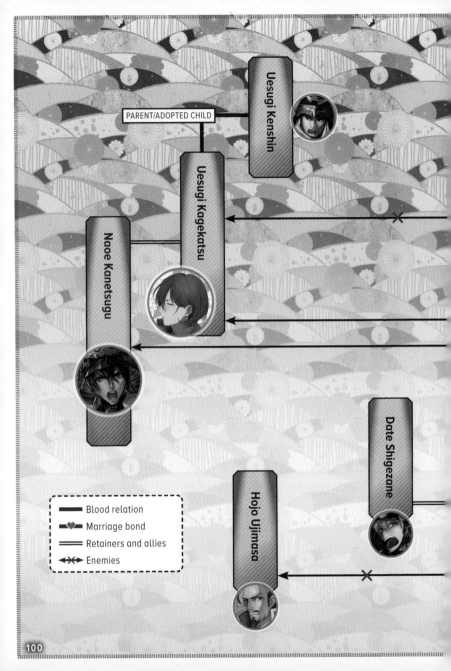

PARENT/ADOPTED CHILD

Uesugi Kenshin

Uesugi Kagekatsu

Naoe Kanetsugu

Date Shigezane

Hojo Ujimasa

Blood relation
Marriage bond
Retainers and allies
Enemies

CHAPTER 5

THE DATE CLAN

AND THEIR RELATIONS

Date Masamune charged his way through the Tohoku region, but he was not fast enough to keep up with Toyotomi Hideyoshi's bid for the throne. In the end, Masamune was defeated.

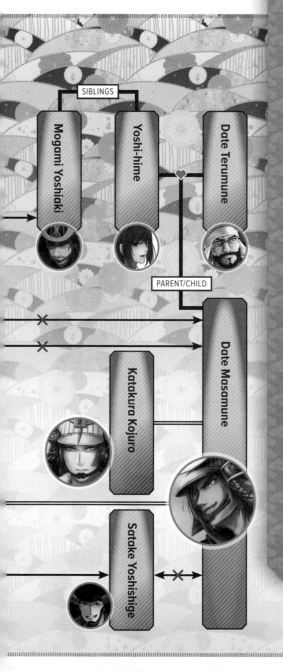

SIBLINGS

Mogami Yoshiaki

Yoshi-hime

Date Terumune

PARENT/CHILD

Katakura Kojuro

Date Masamune

Satake Yoshishige

The One-Eyed Dragon
DATE MASAMUNE

Born: 1567
Died: 1636
Died at age 70 from illness
Birthplace: Dewa Province (present-day Yamagata Prefecture)
Father: Date Terumune
Mother: Yoshi-hime

Main Base

Sendai Castle (Miyagi)

When Date Masamune was young, he came down with a severe illness that almost took his life. In the end, he survived, but he lost his right eye. This did not stop him from becoming a ferocious warrior. He was known—and feared—as "The One-Eyed Dragon."

Masamune became the head of the Date clan when he was 18, and by the time he was 24, he had conquered one-third of the Tohoku region.

At the time, all that stood between Toyotomi Hideyoshi and unification of the nation was the opposition of the Hojo clan. Hideyoshi assembled a huge army for his assault on the clan's stronghold at Odawara Castle, just south of the Date clan's lands. He requested that Masamune join the siege. Young Masamune had his own ambitions to rule the land. For a long time, he would not give Hideyoshi an answer. In the end, he joined the battle on Hideyoshi's side and helped him achieve his dream.

After Hideyoshi's death, Masamune submitted to Tokugawa Ieyasu's reign, fighting against Naoe Kanetsugu in Tohoku.

伊達政宗

A Pardon in Funeral Garb

Masamune was late bringing his troops to the Siege of Odawara, which made Hideyoshi furious. So Masamune dressed like a corpse prepared for cremation. He wore a white kimono and let his hair down from his usual samurai topknot. Hideyoshi was so surprised by this gesture that he unexpectedly pardoned the tardy retainer.

Fighting Strength

Luck

Leadership

Humanity

Willpower

Intelligence

Many believe Masamune could have unified the nation under his own name—if he'd been born sooner.

Masamune's Right-Hand Man
KATAKURA KOJURO

Born: 1557
Died: 1615

Died at age 59 from illness

Birthplace: Dewa Province (present-day Yamagata Prefecture)

Father: Katakura Kageshige

Son: Katakura Shigenaga

Main Base

Shiroishi Castle (Miyagi)

When Katakura Kojuro was 19 years old, he began serving the 9-year-old Date Masamune. The young heir to the Date clan became sick, and his right eye swelled shut. In great pain, Masamune asked Kojuro to take out the infected eye. Kojuro was uncertain at first, but he did as his young master bid him and cut out the eye. The incident brought the two closer together as a test of their mutual trust and bravery. After the loss of his eye, Masamune transformed into a lively and energetic youth, and he grew into a fearsome warrior.

Kojuro's loyal service did not end there. At the Battle of Hitotori Bridge, Masamune found himself surrounded by enemy soldiers, facing certain death. Seeing his lord in mortal danger, Kojuro yelled out his own name, tricking the enemy into thinking that he was Masamune and the real Masamune was his servant. The soldiers, eager to kill the enemy commander, turned and attacked Kojuro instead. Kojuro led them away from his lord, saving Masamune's life.

As his reputation for cleverness and bravery spread, Kojuro was approached by Toyotomi Hideyoshi, who offered him a domain if Kojuro would become one of his retainers. Kojuro flatly refused and remained Masamune's loyal adviser until his death.

片倉小十郎

Kojuro was a loyal aide to Masamune in both politics and battle.

- Fighting Strength
- Luck
- Leadership
- Humanity
- Willpower
- Intelligence

1	2	3	4	5	6	7	8
Oda Clan	Takeda, Uesugi, and Hojo Clans	Toyotomi Clan	Mori Clan	Date Clan	Shimazu, Otomo, and Chosokabe Clans	Tokugawa Clan	Other Samurai

Loyal Supporter of Masamune
DATE SHIGEZANE

伊達成実
（だて しげ ざね）

Born: 1568
Died: 1646
Died at age 79 from illness

Fighting Strength

Luck

Leadership

Humanity

Willpower

Intelligence

Date Shigezane was one of Date Masamune's chief retainers. He fought side by side with Katakura Kojuro in countless battles, where his courage earned him a reputation for never showing fear in the face of the enemy.

Shigezane always said that he would never retreat in battle.

Date Masamune's Neighborhood Rival
MOGAMI YOSHIAKI

最上義光

Born: 1546
Died: 1614
Died at age 69 from illness

Mogami Yoshiaki was one of the most powerful lords of the Warring States period. He arranged a marriage between his younger sister and the powerful Date clan, but there were still constant skirmishes and border disputes. At the Battle of Sekigahara, the western army's Naoe Kanetsugu invaded Yoshiaki's lands, and Yoshiaki emerged victorious.

Fighting Strength

Luck

Leadership

Humanity

Willpower

Intelligence

Yoshiaki fought ferociously to defend his territory.

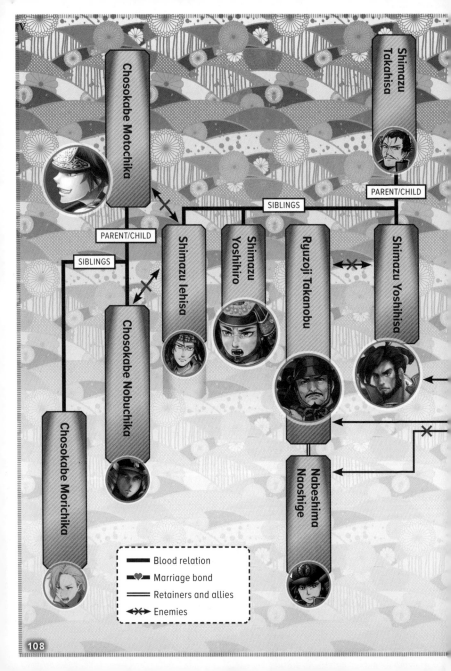

Chosokabe Motochika

Shimazu Takahisa

PARENT/CHILD

SIBLINGS

PARENT/CHILD

Shimazu Iehisa

Shimazu Yoshihiro

Ryuzoji Takanobu

Shimazu Yoshihisa

SIBLINGS

Chosokabe Nobuchika

Chosokabe Morichika

Nabeshima Naoshige

Blood relation
Marriage bond
Retainers and allies
Enemies

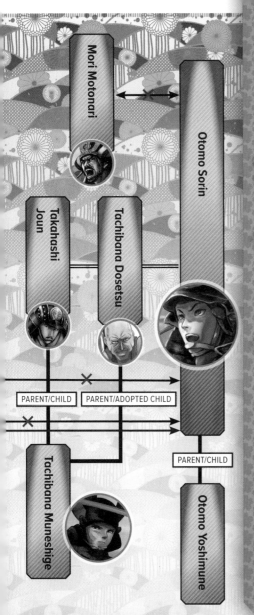

CHAPTER 6

THE SHIMAZU CLAN

THE OTOMO CLAN

THE CHOSOKABE CLAN

AND THEIR RELATIONS

Otomo Sorin amassed great military might across the northern Kyushu region, but when he met the fierce resistance of the Shimazu clan to the south, his ambitions for power . . . were crushed.

1
Oda Clan

2
Takeda, Uesugi, and Hojo Clans

3
Toyotomi Clan

4
Mori Clan

5
Date Clan

6
Shimazu, Otomo, and Chosokabe Clans

7
Tokugawa Clan

8
Other Samurai

Dreams of a United Kyushu Dashed

SHIMAZU YOSHIHISA

Born: 1533
Died: 1611

Died at age 79 from illness

Birthplace: Satsuma Province (present-day Kagoshima Prefecture)

Father: Shimazu Takahisa

Brothers: Shimazu Yoshihiro, Shimazu Toshihisa, Shimazu Iehisa

Main Base

Uchi Castle (Kagoshima)

The eldest son of Shimazu Takahisa, Shimazu Yoshihisa worked alongside his three younger brothers to expand the clan's territory.

Yoshihisa's plans to conquer the entire Kyushu region were off to a good start. He defeated Otomo Sorin's army at the Battle of Mimigawa River and Ryuzoji Takanobu's troops at the Battle of Okitanawate, making the Shimazu clan the most powerful in the Kyushu region. His string of victories continued with the capture of Iwaya Castle in Fukuoka. The dream of unifying Kyushu under one banner was within his grasp. But when news of this rising power in the west reached Toyotomi Hideyoshi in Kyoto, Hideyoshi was not happy.

Hideyoshi sent an army of 200,000 soldiers to thwart the growing danger. Yoshihisa knew he wouldn't win, so he surrendered to Hideyoshi and accepted the condition that he become a Buddhist monk. Hideyoshi allowed him to rule the Satsuma region, and the Shimazu clan survived.

Fighting
Strength

Luck

Leadership

Humanity

Willpower

Intelligence

島津義久

Yoshihisa raised his clan to its
greatest heights but knew when
to surrender.

United His Family

SHIMAZU TAKAHISA

島津貴久

Born: 1514
Died: 1571
Died at age 58 from illness

After watching the branches of the Shimazu family fight over their territories, Shimazu Takahisa led his army and unified Satsuma Province, achieving his dream of becoming a full feudal lord.

Fighting Strength

Luck

Leadership

Humanity

Willpower

Intelligence

Takahisa was a great unifier, with interests in firearms and Christianity.

112

Legendary Charge at Sekigahara
SHIMAZU YOSHIHIRO

Born: 1535
Died: 1619
Died at
age 85
from illness

島
津
義
弘

Shimazu Yoshihiro was the son
of Shimazu Takahisa and the
brother of Shimazu Yoshihisa. He
was on the front lines fighting
against Toyotomi Hideyoshi. But
after Yoshihisa had to surrender,
Yoshihiro helped Hideyoshi unify
the nation.

Yoshihiro and his soldiers
fought as part of the western
army at the Battle of Sekigahara.
Despite the army's defeat,
Yoshihiro charged through the
center of the eastern army and
lived to tell the tale!

Fighting Strength

Luck

Leadership

Humanity

Willpower

Intelligence

Yoshihiro was an expert swordsman.
He created masterful battle plans
and was beloved by his retainers.

113

Another Contender for the Title

OTOMO SORIN

Born: 1530
Died: 1587
Died at age 58 from illness

大友宗麟

Fighting Strength

Luck

Leadership

Humanity

Willpower

Intelligence

Skilled at diplomacy and making valuable alliances, Sorin traded with Europe and China.

Otomo Sorin was one of the few feudal lords who converted to Christianity. He used the power of his retainers to expand the clan's territory, eventually controlling the other lords in the Kyushu region and even in Iyo Province in Shikoku.

Sorin was the most powerful ruler in Kyushu—until he ran up against the Shimazu clan. One by one, Sorin lost his domains.

114

God of Thunder
TACHIBANA DOSETSU

Born: 1513
Died: 1585
Died at age 73 from illness

立花道雪

Tachibana Dosetsu was a retainer of the Otomo clan. After being struck by lightning, he lost the use of his left leg. He would ride out to battle on a platform and sit in the center of the battlefield, commanding his troops. They called him "God of Thunder." His unflinching presence on the field encouraged them to fight harder. With Dosetsu's help, Otomo Sorin was able to expand his influence to the south.

Fighting Strength

Luck

Leadership

Humanity

Willpower

Intelligence

Dosetsu was a brave general who kept his young lord, Sorin, on the path of righteousness.

The Bravest Man in Kyushu
TACHIBANA MUNESHIGE

立花宗茂

Born: 1567
Died: 1642
Died at age 76 from illness

When his father died, Tachibana Muneshige was adopted by Tachibana Dosetsu and became a retainer of the Otomo clan. He drove the Shimazu army out of Chikuzen Province and became one of Toyotomi Hideyoshi's retainers. He fought against the Shimazu clan in the Kyushu region and participated in the invasion of Korea.

Muneshige lost at the Battle of Sekigahara, but Tokugawa Ieyasu made Muneshige a feudal lord after the war.

- Fighting Strength
- Luck
- Leadership
- Humanity
- Willpower
- Intelligence

Muneshige was recognized by all as a man of character, skilled in martial arts and fine arts alike.

116

✤ A Tale of Two Hands

Kuroda Nagamasa distinguished himself at the Battle of Sekigahara. Afterward, Tokugawa Ieyasu shook his hand to thank him. When Nagamasa told his father (Kuroda Kambe), Kambe glared at his son and said, "What were you doing with your other hand?" Kambe was telling his son that, if he had stabbed Ieyasu in that instant, he could have taken the throne for himself.

✤ Mitsunari's Three Cups of Conscientious Tea

Toyotomi Hideyoshi trusted Ishida Mitsunari completely, but their first meeting was a little unusual. When Mitsunari was a boy, he worked at a temple. One day, Hideyoshi stopped in and said he was thirsty. Mitsunari brought him a cup of cool tea so Hideyoshi could drink it quickly. When Hideyoshi asked for a second cup, Mitsunari brought out slightly warmer tea. When he asked for a third, the boy brought out a cup of hot tea so he could warm back up. Impressed by the boy's attention to detail, Hideyoshi brought him back to the castle.

✤ Even Free Spirits Feared Kagekatsu

Maeda Keiji was famous for his garish clothes and his colorful pranks and antics, which respected neither rank nor station. The only person he seemed to fear was Uesugi Kagekatsu, who was rumored to never laugh or even smile. One night Keiji was attending a banquet with many powerful generals, so he put on a monkey mask and danced around, sitting on the generals' laps and making jokes. He went around the room playing pranks on everyone there. The only lap he wouldn't sit on was Kagekatsu's.

The Cleverest
GENERALS

[Mori Motonari]

Mori Motonari married his second son into the Kikkawa clan and his third son into the Kobayakawa clan, consolidating influence without starting any wars. When he did go to battle, he used smart tactics to secure victory after victory until the Mori clan was among the most powerful in Japan.

Used Strategy to Dominate

[Sanada Masayuki]

Sanada Masayuki is famous for defeating the mighty Tokugawa army not once but twice. He lured the army to Ueda Castle, where his 2,000 defenders defeated an army of 7,000. When the humiliated Tokugawa troops returned for revenge with 38,000 soldiers, Masayuki still won the day with just 3,500—less than one-tenth of his enemy's force!

Brought Tokugawa's Army to Its Knees—Twice

"Battle's not just about running around swinging your sword. You have to use your head!"

[Takenaka Hambe]

Takenaka Hambe became known as a master of ensnaring his enemy. He would instruct his soldiers to hide, letting the enemy overrun their position. Then Hambe's troops would leap out for a surprise attack. He used this technique many times, famously defeating Oda Nobunaga's army when he was a samurai of the Saito clan.

Skilled at Ensnaring

[Kuroda Kambe]

Kuroda Kambe was not afraid to try unconventional battle strategies. He cut off supply chains and access to water when a direct attack would be too difficult. His ability to outthink other generals was so great that Toyotomi Hideyoshi predicted that after his death, Kambe would be the person who would take the throne from his heirs.

Even Hideyoshi Feared His Tactics

[Yamamoto Kansuke]

Yamamoto Kansuke was knowledgeable, not only in the ways of battle but also in reconnaissance tactics, castle construction, and other skills that helped him greatly expand the territory of the Takeda clan. He was so skillful that people started using the new word "Yamakan" (a combination of his first and last names) to mean "a clever tactician."

Shingen's Right-Hand Man

The Demon Baby

CHOSOKABE MOTOCHIKA

Born: 1539
Died: 1599
Died at age 61 from illness
Birthplace: Tosa Province (present-day Kochi Prefecture)
Father: Chosokabe Kunichika
Sons: Chosokabe Nobuchika, Chosokabe Morichika

Main Base

Oko Castle (Kochi)

Chosokabe Motochika was born to a family of samurai that ruled a part of Tosa Province. As a child, some people called him "Princess Baby" because of his fair coloring. Later, he showed great bravery in expanding his territory and became known as "the Demon Baby."

Oda Nobunaga felt threatened by Motochika and his ability. He was on his way to attack Motochika's castle, when he was killed at Honnoji Temple.

After that, Motochika expanded his territory even farther. He eventually ruled over the entire Shikoku region. However, his glory ended when Toyotomi Hideyoshi attacked him with an army of 120,000 troops. Motochika surrendered and ended up as the lord of Tosa.

Fighting Strength

Luck

Leadership

Humanity

Willpower

Intelligence

Motochika was famous for his bravery and skill with a spear. He was also known for his generosity, honesty, and loyalty.

120

長宗我部元親

Handsome Young General
CHOSOKABE NOBUCHIKA

**Born: 1565
Died: 1586
Died at age 22 in battle**

長宗我部信親

Chosokabe Nobuchika was the eldest son of Chosokabe Motochika. He was known for his intelligence and good looks. He and his father joined Toyotomi Hideyoshi's invasion of the Kyushu region with great expectations. But at the Battle of Hetsugi River, Nobuchika's encampment was surprised by an ambush, and he died during the battle.

Fighting Strength

Luck

Leadership

Humanity

Willpower

Intelligence

Nobuchika was intelligent, brave, and popular with his men.

Teacher Turned General
CHOSOKABE MORICHIKA

Born: 1575
Died: 1615
Executed at
age 41

長宗我部盛親

Chosokabe Morichika was the fourth son of Chosokabe Motochika. He led the clan after the death of his brother Chosokabe Nobuchika. He fought for the western army at the Battle of Sekigahara. After they lost, Tokugawa Ieyasu greatly reduced the clan's lands. Morichika became a teacher.

When Morichika learned that the Toyotomi clan were making their final stand at Osaka Castle against Ieyasu, he joined the fight. They lost, and Ieyasu put Morichika and his sons to death.

Fighting Strength

Luck

Leadership

Humanity

Willpower

Intelligence

Morichika's ferocity at the Battle of Osaka earned him widespread attention.

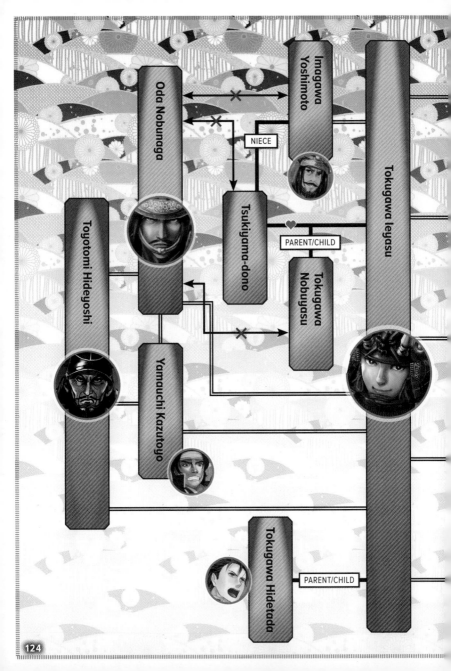

Imagawa Yoshimoto

Oda Nobunaga

NIECE

Tsukiyama-dono

PARENT/CHILD

Tokugawa Nobuyasu

Tokugawa Ieyasu

Toyotomi Hideyoshi

Yamauchi Kazutoyo

Tokugawa Hidetada

PARENT/CHILD

CHAPTER 7

THE TOKUGAWA CLAN

AND THEIR RELATIONS

With the deaths of Oda Nobunaga and Toyotomi Hideyoshi, Tokugawa Ieyasu inched toward the throne, supported along the way by his powerful samurai.

Sakai Tadatsugu

Honda Tadakatsu

Ii Naomasa

Sakakibara Yasumasa

Hattori Hanzo

━━━ Blood relation
💜 Marriage bond
═══ Retainers and allies
◄►◄► Enemies

Shogun of United Japan

TOKUGAWA IEYASU

Born: 1542
Died: 1616
Died at age 75 from illness
Birthplace: Mikawa Province (present-day Aichi Prefecture)
Father: Matsudaira Hirotada
Sons: Matsudaira Nobuyasu, Tokugawa Hidetada

Main Base

Edo Castle (Tokyo)

Tokugawa Ieyasu was born into the Matsudaira clan, which was ruled by the more powerful Imagawa clan. After Oda Nobunaga defeated the Imagawa clan, Ieyasu formed an alliance with him. But in reality, the Matsudaira clan became servants of the Oda clan. Ieyasu changed his name from Matsudaira to the more noble-sounding Tokugawa and bided his time.

After Nobunaga's death, Ieyasu went head-to-head against Toyotomi Hideyoshi. Once again, he decided to submit to a powerful foe rather than destroy himself by fighting. Hideyoshi sent Ieyasu to the Kanto region, away from the center of power in Kyoto. But while he ruled in Hideyoshi's name, Ieyasu was using his position as the head of the Council of Elders to consolidate his own power.

In 1598, Hideyoshi died, and Ieyasu made his move. He allied himself with powerful generals and, at the Battle of Sekigahara, he defeated Ishida Mitsunari, the other contender for the throne.

Ieyasu moved the seat of power from Kyoto to Edo (present-day Tokyo) and declared himself the new shogun. He lived just long enough to see his troops victorious at the Battle of Osaka, which marked the end of the Toyotomi clan.

徳川家康

Fighting Strength

Luck

Leadership

Humanity

Willpower

Intelligence

Not a fierce fighter, Ieyasu polished his skills and learned to use the strength of others for his own goals.

127

1	2	3	4	5	6	7	8
Oda Clan	Takeda, Uesugi, and Hojo Clans	Toyotomi Clan	Mori Clan	Date Clan	Shimazu, Otomo, and Chosokabe Clans	Tokugawa Clan	Other Samurai

A Natural Leader
TOKUGAWA HIDETADA

Born: 1579
Died: 1632
Died at age 54 from illness

徳川秀忠

Fighting Strength

Luck

Leadership

Humanity

Willpower

Intelligence

Hidetada was an honest leader who built the foundations of a dynasty.

Tokugawa Hidetada was Tokugawa Ieyasu's third son. After his father's death, Hidetada became shogun and displayed a natural ability to rule. His good governance laid the foundation for a long and stable dynasty that governed Japan for the next 250 years.

The Leader of the Heavenly Kings
SAKAI TADATSUGU

Born: 1527
Died: 1596
Died at age 70 from illness

酒井忠次

Sakai Tadatsugu was the chief member of Tokugawa Ieyasu's "Four Heavenly Kings," who were at Ieyasu's side for all of his clan's most important battles.

Tadatsugu's greatest regret was that he was unable to save the life of Ieyasu's first son, Nobuyasu. Nobuyasu was a hostage of Oda Nobunaga to ensure Ieyasu's loyalty. When Nobunaga began to suspect Ieyasu of treason, he ordered Nobuyasu to take his own life. Tadatsugu tried to convince his master to change his mind, but he could not.

Fighting Strength

Luck

Leadership

Humanity

Willpower

Intelligence

Tadatsugu was so strong and wise that Nobunaga said he must have eyes in the back of his head.

The Fiercest Fighter in the East
HONDA TADAKATSU

Born: 1548
Died: 1610
Died at age 63 from illness
Birthplace: Mikawa Province (present-day Aichi Prefecture)
Father: Honda Tadataka
Children: Honda Tadamasa, Komatsu-hime (wife of Sanada Nobuyuki)

Main Base

Otaki Castle (Chiba)

One of Tokugawa Ieyasu's "Four Heavenly Kings," and certainly the most heroic, Honda Tadakatsu was known for his unsurpassed skills with a spear. Toyotomi Hideyoshi nicknamed him "the Fiercest Fighter in the East."

Tadakatsu became one of Ieyasu's samurai at a very young age, fighting his first battle at 13. At the Battle of Anegawa River, he led a charge that broke the enemy ranks and defeated the Asakura army—and he was the only one charging! He had another famous victory at the Battle of Hitokotozaka Hill, when the army of the Takeda clan attacked Ieyasu's troops from the rear. Tadakatsu led his soldiers to stop the assault and drive them off, famously saying that it wasn't worth Ieyasu's time to stop and fight an army like the Takeda clan's.

In the lead-up to the Battle of Sekigahara, Tadakatsu proved that he had brains to go with his brawn by sending letters to the most powerful lords throughout the land, convincing them to join Ieyasu's army.

He fought in 57 battles over the course of his lifetime, and he never once got so much as a scratch.

本多忠勝

Fighting Strength

Luck

Leadership

Humanity

Willpower

Intelligence

Tadakatsu was praised for his strength and strategy by the most famous generals in Japan—and by his foes too!

The Red Devil of Ii
II NAOMASA

Born: 1561
Died: 1602
Died at age 42 from illness
Birthplace: Totomi Province (present-day Shizuoka Prefecture)
Father: Ii Naochika
Son: Ii Naotaka

Main Base

Sawayama Castle (Shiga)

From a young age, Ii Naomasa was one of Tokugawa Ieyasu's most trusted samurai. At the Battle of Komaki and Nagakute, he led 2,000 soldiers, all wearing red armor. Wielding an enormous spear, he scattered the enemy troops while cutting deep into Toyotomi Hideyoshi's lines.

Alongside Honda Tadakatsu, Naomasa was one of the top generals at the Battle of Sekigahara. He led Ieyasu's troops to victory. After the battle, he negotiated terms of surrender with the most powerful lords in the losing army and helped establish a stable political base for the Tokugawa shoguns.

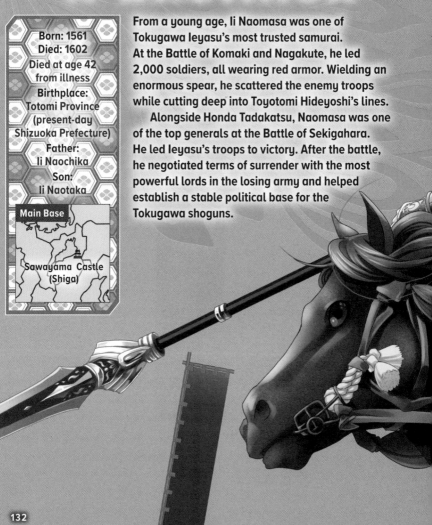

井伊直政

Fighting Strength

Luck

Leadership

Humanity

Willpower

Intelligence

A skillful fighter and diplomat, Naomasa
left a legacy with sword
and pen alike.

133

Leader of the Iga Ninja
HATTORI HANZO

服部半蔵

> **Born: 1542**
> **Died: 1596**
> **Died at age 55 from illness**

Fighting Strength

Luck — Leadership

Humanity

Willpower

Intelligence

Hanzo had the leadership and fighting skills required to unite the ninja.

Hattori Hanzo was born with the more typical name Masanari. As the leader of the Iga ninjas, he participated in countless battles. After the betrayal at Honnoji Temple, Hanzo was responsible for protecting Tokugawa Ieyasu from suffering the same fate as Oda Nobunaga and transporting him safely back to Okazaki Castle. He continued to protect Ieyasu and his family during their rise to ultimate power.

He Had a Secret Helper— His Wife, Chiyo

YAMAUCHI KAZUTOYO

山内一豊

Yamauchi Kazutoyo used his wife Chiyo's savings to buy one of the most famous horses in the country. The horse caught Oda Nobunaga's eye and put Kazutoyo in the spotlight. Later, when serving under Toyotomi Hideyoshi, Kazutoyo played an important role in unifying the nation.

After Hideyoshi's death, Kazutoyo served under Tokugawa Ieyasu. Chiyo learned that Ishida Mitsunari was raising an army to challenge Ieyasu. Kazutoyo gave his lord this information and his castle to use, and Ieyasu later rewarded him with Tosa Province.

- Fighting Strength
- Luck
- Leadership
- Humanity
- Willpower
- Intelligence

Kazutoyo's wife helped him serve the most powerful men in the land and survive the Warring States period.

Kani Saizo

Matsunaga Hisahide

Todo Takatora

Sakuma Morimasa

CHAPTER 8

OTHER SAMURAI

TRUE TO THEMSELVES

More than the throne or even their clans, some samurai lived for the glory of their own skill in battle. They changed loyalties when it suited them, they disobeyed orders when they didn't like them, and their fighting spirit was a powerful force that ran throughout the entire era.

Araki Murashige

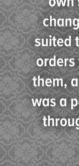

Gamo Ujisato

Explosive Resistance

MATSUNAGA HISAHIDE

Born: 1510 (?)
Died: 1577
Died at age 68 (?) by his own hand

松永久秀

Very little is known about Matsunaga Hisahide's early life. He served as a retainer to Oda Nobunaga but eventually had a falling out with him. Nobunaga offered him a deal: Send out your most famous pottery and I will spare you. Rather than submit either his treasured pottery or his life, Hisahide filled a clay pot with gunpowder and exploded it like a grenade, killing himself and destroying his castle.

Fighting Strength

Luck

Leadership

Humanity

Willpower

Intelligence

Hisahide is remembered as an evil man who killed the Ashikaga shogun, set fire to Todaiji Temple, and betrayed Nobunaga.

138

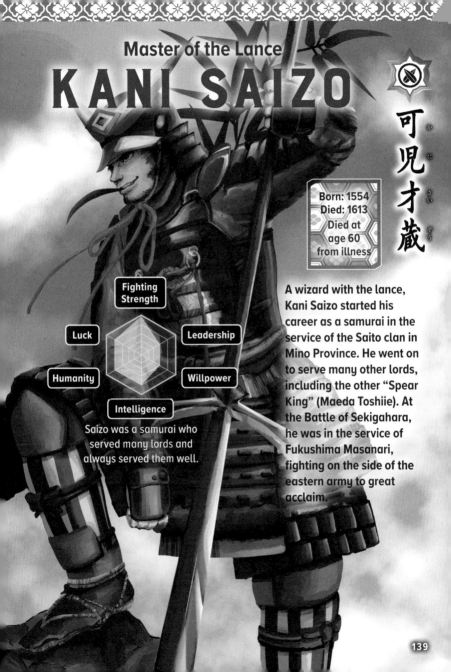

Master of the Lance
KANI SAIZO

可児才蔵

**Born: 1554
Died: 1613
Died at age 60 from illness**

Fighting Strength

Luck

Leadership

Humanity

Willpower

Intelligence

Saizo was a samurai who served many lords and always served them well.

A wizard with the lance, Kani Saizo started his career as a samurai in the service of the Saito clan in Mino Province. He went on to serve many other lords, including the other "Spear King" (Maeda Toshiie). At the Battle of Sekigahara, he was in the service of Fukushima Masanari, fighting on the side of the eastern army to great acclaim.

1	2	3	4	5	6	7	8
Oda Clan	Takeda, Uesugi, and Hojo Clans	Toyotomi Clan	Mori Clan	Date Clan	Shimazu, Otomo, and Chosokabe Clans	Tokugawa Clan	Other Samurai

A Demon on the Battlefield

SAKUMA MORIMASA

Born: 1554
Died: 1583
Executed at age 30

佐久間盛政

Sakuma Morimasa was a giant of a warrior who started as samurai to Oda Nobunaga. After Nobunaga's death, Morimasa became samurai to his uncle, Shibata Katsuie. At the Battle of Shizugatake, he charged directly into the heart of Toyotomi Hideyoshi's army and was captured. The battle was lost. Impressed with Morimasa's valor, Hideyoshi offered to take him on as one of his own samurai, but Morimasa chose to die instead.

Fighting Strength

Luck

Leadership

Humanity

Willpower

Intelligence

Morimasa made his name with his sword.

140

TODO TAKATORA

藤堂高虎

Fighting Strength

Luck · Leadership · Humanity · Willpower · Intelligence

Takatora was a skilled warrior who worked hard so long as he felt he had a master worth fighting for.

Todo Takatora is famous for saying that changing masters seven times is what made him a true samurai. But the truth is that he changed masters more than 10 times! He started as a samurai of the Azai clan. Toyotomi Hideyoshi was his seventh master. Takatora was an admiral in the invasion of Korea, and after Hideyoshi's death, he went on to serve Tokugawa Ieyasu and Tokugawa Hidetada.

Born: 1556
Died: 1630
Died at age 75 from illness

141

Betrayed Nobunaga, Lost a Family

ARAKI MURASHIGE

**Born: 1535
Died: 1586
Died at age 52
from illness**

荒木村重

Araki Murashige did great service for Oda Nobunaga as one of his retainers, until the Mori clan convinced him to betray his master. He holed up in Arioka Castle for 10 months and then fled for the protection of the Moris, leaving behind his wife and children. When Nobunaga finally recaptured the castle, he took his revenge by killing Murashige's family, retainers, and anyone else he found in the castle—nearly 600 people.

Fighting Strength

Luck

Leadership

Humanity

Willpower

Intelligence

Murashige had strength and promise, but his military career died along with his family.

Lord of Aizu

GAMO UJISATO

蒲生氏郷

Born: 1556
Died: 1595
Died at age 40 from illness

As a boy, Gamo Ujisato was given to Oda Nobunaga as a hostage to ensure his family's loyalty. Nobunaga recognized his value, and Ujisato married Nobunaga's daughter. Later, he served Toyotomi Hideyoshi. He was sent to conquer Ise Province and was made lord of Aizu Province when Hideyoshi unified the nation at last.

Fighting Strength

Luck

Leadership

Humanity

Willpower

Intelligence

Ujisato was trusted and relied on by Nobunaga and Hideyoshi for his strength and intelligence.

143

GLOSSARY

clan: a family, or a group united by common characteristics or interests

feudal: relating to feudalism, a system of governance where a person or family owned much of the land in an area and ruled over all the people who lived on that land

matchlock: a type of musket (early rifle) that used a slow-burning match to ignite the charge that would fire the weapon

musket: an early shoulder gun used by soldiers

musketeer: a soldier armed with a musket

retainer: a person in service to another

seppuku: taking one's life for honor, by stabbing oneself deeply in the gut; also called *hara-kiri*

shogun: a military governor ruling Japan before 1867

RESOURCES

Want to learn more? Keep reading about samurai, ninja, and ancient Japan!

BOOKS

All About Japan—Stories, Songs, Crafts, and Games for Kids by Willamarie Moore (Tuttle Publishing, 2017).

Hands-On History! Ancient Japan: Step Back to the Time of Shoguns and Samurai by Fiona MacDonald (Armadillo, 2014).

How to Be a Samurai Warrior by Fiona MacDonald (National Geographic Children's Books, 2007).

The Ninja Handbook by Yuji Yamada (Gakken, 2018).

Ninjas and Samurai: A Nonfiction Companion to Magic Tree House #5 by Mary Pope Osborne and Natalie Pope Boyce (Random House Books for Young Readers, 2014).

Real Samurai by Stephen Turnbull (Enchanted Lion Publishing, 2007).

Samurai: Warriors Around the World by Jeanne Nagle (Rosen Publishing, 2017).

Samurai Science by Marcia Amidon Lusted (Capstone Press, 2016).

You Wouldn't Want to Be a Samurai!: A Deadly Career You'd Rather Not Pursue by Fiona MacDonald (Scholastic, 2009).

WEBSITES

National Geographic
kids.nationalgeographic.com/explore/countries/japan

Japanese Folk Tales
web-japan.org/kidsweb/folk/index.html